A Guide To
MUSICAL
ACOUSTICS

H. LOWERY
M.Ed., Ph.D., D.Sc., F.T.C.L.

Principal of South West Essex Technical College,
London

DOVER PUBLICATIONS, INC., NEW YORK

This Dover edition, first published in 1966, is an unabridged and corrected republication of the work originally published by Dennis Dobson in 1956.

This edition is published by special arrangement with Dobson Books, Ltd., 80 Kensington Church Street, London W. 8, England.

Library of Congress Catalog Card Number: 66-20422

Manufactured in the United States of America
Dover Publications, Inc.
180 Varick Street
New York, N. Y. 10014

CONTENTS

PREFACE

The late Sir Percy Buck, in his little book entitled *Acoustics for Musicians* (Oxford University Press), reminded us that for the understanding of the principles of the subject, certain mathematical and physical conceptions cannot be avoided. This physical basis has often led writers on acoustics to produce scientific works that seem to have little connection with the art of music. It is hardly surprising therefore that the subject should have been so unpopular among musicians in the past.

Nor did the traditional treatment of acoustics in the music examinations of the universities help matters. Conundrums with little reference to music were all too common. Thus nothing can be said for an examination question in which the candidate for the Bachelor of Music degree was required to discuss the significance of the ratio of the specific heats of gases in the theoretical calculation of the velocity of sound in air. In many universities the music student was required to attend the lectures on sound forming part of the degree course in physics and to pass the corresponding physics examination. Happily this condition is being remedied by the provision of *ad hoc* courses in musical acoustics but there is no doubt of the harm that it did to the proper appreciation of the value of acoustical knowledge.

Most of the elementary physical ideas are given in Chapter II of the present work where they are presented in as simple a form as possible suitable for reference purposes. Modern Musical Acoustics is however not by any means entirely a matter of mathematics and physics. Dealing as it does with the practical side of music, it leans heavily on psychology; much of its content is descriptive in character with examples drawn from the reader's own experience in music making. Tone production by the various musical instruments, the objective conditions of musical expression, the effect of the concert hall upon performance, the reproduction of music, the nature of musical scales, the rôle of the ear in musical perception— these and many other practical matters come within its purview.

It is hoped that the following chapters may serve to interest the student, teacher, and practising musician in some of the most fundamental factors in the nature of music. For the student taking an examination in Musical Acoustics, a selection of specimen questions is appended. A short Bibliography of suggestions for further reading is also provided.

H.L.

I

MUSIC AND ACOUSTICS

'The special educational value of this combined study of music and acoustics is that more than almost any other study it involves a continued appeal to what we must observe ourselves. The facts are things which must be felt; they cannot be learned from any description of them.'

Clerk Maxwell

What is Acoustics?

Of Acoustics, Grove's *Dictionary of Music* says—'the science of hearing, commonly includes all that relates to the physical basis of sound on which the art of music rests'. The term has however at various times been used to cover (a) the branch of Physics called *sound*, (b) the science of hearing, and (c) the physical basis of music.

Again, the term *sound* itself has two well-defined meanings, namely, (a) the sensation of hearing, and (b) the external stimulus of sensation, the latter covering the vibrations of the sounding body, the transmission of sound energy by waves in a medium, and the properties of those waves. In this sense any connection there may be with music is far from evident.

In recent years, the content of acoustics has been greatly widened through the development of numerous electrical devices for the production, reproduction and radio-transmission of sound, all of which have considerable bearing on the practice of music. These new fields are sometimes designated *applied acoustics, electro-acoustics,* or even *acoustical engineering.* Psychology has also added a substantial contribution which has completely transformed the scope and applications of the subject and placed the physical data in an entirely new setting.

Acoustics and Music

Sounds are obviously the basic material of music, but it does not follow that the practising musician, whether he be composer or performer, must necessarily possess a competent knowledge of the nature of sounds before he can set to work. Tovey used to say that Beethoven probably knew nothing of acoustics. Moreover it is difficult to see what musical use Paganini could have made of the information that in tuning his violin strings he was making adjustments in accordance with the law that 'the frequency of vibration of a string is directly proportional to the square root of its tension'. Often in the history of music the performer has anticipated the scientist, thus Tartini on his violin discovered difference tones without scientific aid while Paganini evolved many complexities in the production of harmonics which baffled the scientific writers of the time. (An eye-witness of a concert given by Paganini in the Old Ship Hotel, Brighton, wrote to a friend that the violinist did incredible feats; the pitches of the notes continued to rise though the left hand actually moved away from the body of the violin. This may be explained by Paganini's peculiar uses of harmonics.)

That music is not a physical but a mental phenomenon and that therefore *musical acoustics* involves psychological as well as physical laws is something that has only been recently recognised.

The physicist and the musician look at sounds from two entirely different points of view. Whereas the physicist is concerned with *a single sound* and all that goes to its production, the musician *qua* musician is concerned almost entirely with *relations between sounds*—a mental act.

Jeans provides a good example of this. In his *Science and Music* he records that experiments with the cathode ray oscillograph show that the master pianist has no greater range of effects at his disposal in playing a single note on the piano than has a child. To generalise from this and say (as some have done) that the untemperamental scientist has debunked all piano teaching amounts to nonsense and indicates complete ignorance of the essential nature of music itself. The fact is that *the musician is not concerned with single tones;* music only begins when one tone is related to another. Of course the scientist, and for that matter commonsense, tells us that if we strike the piano key hard we get a loud and brilliant tone and further he can tell us how it comes about that the tone is more brilliant (namely by the development of high-pitched overtones) but the information is of no musical value until the relation of the tone in question to other tones becomes known. Clearly the second tone may be louder or softer than the first tone or longer or shorter in duration, indeed the subtle difference in loudness and time duration between series of tones makes possible an unlimited range of interpretative effects.

It is when we leave purely musical questions and discuss the structure and properties of instruments that physical knowledge comes into its own in acoustics. The number of general principles involved is however surprisingly small. Moreover, it has to be admitted that even when physical theory has done its best the result is often of only slight technical value. No one ever heard of an organ builder who voiced the pipes of an organ according to scientific theory despite the volume of mathematical and physical theory on the vibration of the air in pipes. Here we must observe that frequently all science can do is to show in a general way *how* things work. It should not specify the way in which they ought to work. This is an important matter with serious potentialities and in those few cases where science is in a position to specify, the specification should be continually subjected to musical controls, as we shall see in discussing the acoustics of concert rooms.

The Principle of Tonal Relatedness

New views on the nature of music enable us to put the subject of acoustics in its proper perspective as an element in musical education. Probably the connotation of the old term will be difficult to change but little confusion will result if we use the term *musical acoustics* to cover not only the physical aspects of tone production but all the relevant psychological phenomena as well, bearing in mind that music is essentially concerned with the relatedness of tones.

This relatedness is obvious enough in melody and harmony; in the former it is customary to speak of the rise and fall in the pitch of the notes and the term melodic curve (or contour) is in frequent use to designate it, hence it is clear that the emphasis is not upon one note but upon the connection between that note and what notes have preceded and followed it. When it is said that the melody reaches a climax we do not mean that a given note is particularly important but that the whole series of notes preceding it have shown a tendency to rise in pitch up to its level and the notes immediately following it tend to decrease in pitch—it is the *change* in the pitches of the notes that matters, not the actual pitches of the notes. The progressive change is the musician's concern, the actual pitches are the physicist's concern. Similarly, in musical intervals and chords the musician is interested only in the aural effect produced by the notes sounding

simultaneously while in sequences of chords the constituent notes of any individual chord are not matters of
arbitrary selection but are determined entirely by what
precedes and follows them.

The importance of this relatedness in music—which,
be it noted, is essentially mental in character—cannot be
too strongly insisted upon. At once, it discriminates between musical acoustics on one hand and the physical
phenomena of sound on the other. Many matters such as
the mechanics of vibration, the mode of propagation of
sound waves in solid, liquid and gaseous media, the
physiology of the ear together with many other topics in
the theory of sound thus become incidentals only, while
those that still remain of importance such as the scale,
consonance and dissonance, and the tuning of musical
instruments are viewed from a new standpoint.

II

THE MATERIAL OF MUSIC

'There's music in the sighing of a reed;
There's music in the gushing of a rill;'
(Byron: *Don Juan*)

Sound

The elementary phenomena of sound are very well familiar to us in everyday life. Thus it is a matter of common observation that many sounding bodies are in a state of vibration, that is, their parts are moving rapidly to-and-fro. If we touch the edge of a large bell or the diaphragm of a drum while it is sounding, the tremulous movements can actually be felt. Again, the strings of a violin may be seen to perform motions backwards and forwards when bowed. It is not surprising therefore to learn that *all* sounds may be traced back to a body in a state of vibration. Furthermore, while the body is vibrating, we experience the sensation of sound due to the ear registering variations of pressure which have been communicated to it through the air from the local disturbances produced round the vibrating source. These pressure variations may be picked up by a microphone, amplified and registered on a cathode ray tube (similar to the tube of a television set) and provide a convenient means of studying the complexity of the corresponding sounds. (See the Figures on page 47).

The science of sound, a branch of physics, is concerned with the physical aspects of all the above phenomena, namely, the character of the to-and-fro movements of the

14

source, the mode of transmission of the vibratory disturbance through the medium (in this case the air) between the vibrating source and the ear, and the production of the sensation of sound in the ear. Strictly speaking, the physical phenomena terminate when the auditory nerve is stimulated, for at that stage the mind takes over the interpretation of the incoming data and the study becomes psychological rather than physical. Indeed, sound is a borderland study and some topics such as the musical scale may be advantageously discussed from both physical and psychological points of view. In connection with pure hearing, there is also a physiological aspect to be considered but we shall not be concerned with this in any major sense.

Vibrations

All sounds originate from a body in a state of vibration. So important is this fact that we must go into it in some detail. In order to make clear our ideas let us consider the movements of the free end of a long, thin strip of metal, for example, a steel rule, securely fixed at the other end between the jaws of a vice. The strip possesses considerable flexibility. When the free end is displaced to one side and let go it will tend to return to its original position but in doing so will acquire so much momentum that it will over-shoot its normal steady position and ultimately reach an extreme position on the other side. The conditions are now the opposite of those that formerly prevailed and the movements of the strip will thus be reversed, resulting in a to-and-fro movement of the free end. Without some continuously applied external driving force the excursions of the strip on either side of the normal position will become less and less until it finally comes to rest in the central position. During its movement, the strip is said to vibrate.

If we concentrate on some single point of the strip, for example, a point on the free end, this point will be seen to perform the same or nearly the same series of movements over and over again. This is the feature which characterises vibratory movement. The maximum distance any vibrating point moves from its position of rest is called the *amplitude* of the vibration.

The number of to-and-fro movements made each second by the strip is called the *frequency* of vibration. The *time* taken from *one side to the other and back again* is the *period* of the motion and although the magnitude of the excursions on each side of the normal becomes less and less as mentioned above, the period remains the same and the movement is said to be *isochronous.*

A simple pendulum provides another very good example of such isochronous movement. If a small sphere of metal, called the bob, is suspended by a long thread from a fixed point and displaced a short distance to one side of the vertical through the point, on being liberated it will perform isochronous vibrations. If n represents the number of vibrations made each second and t is the period or time of each complete vibration, then $n \times t = 1$ second or, $n = \frac{1}{t}$.

It should be noted that no sound is heard from a simple pendulum nor from the strip of metal vibrating as was described for moderate lengths. This is because the ear only registers as sounds those frequencies that lie between about 20 and 20,000 vibrations per second. These limits are called the *thresholds of audibility,* their exact values varying slightly from individual to individual. Thus if the strip were moving to-and-fro only three times a second, no sound would be heard. If the length of the strip projecting from the vice were progressively decreased in length, the frequency would increase and at a certain value a low pitched murmur would be heard which would rise in pitch the greater the number of vibrations made per second, for *the frequency determines the pitch of the note.*

A common source of sound is the tuning fork which may be regarded as an extension of the use of the metal strip considered above. The fork consists of two strips of metal, the prongs, free at one end but united into the shank at the other end. The prongs move inwards and outwards together with a frequency sufficiently great to produce a sound. The sound may be intensified by pressing the shank on an extended surface such as a table top which has the effect of causing a greater quantity of air to be acted upon than when the fork is suspended freely in the air. Other sources of vibration to be noticed are the strings of the violin family of instruments and of the harp and piano, the air in a flute or organ pipe, the reed in the oboe or bassoon, the skin of a drum, the vocal cords of the human voice, the player's lips in brass instruments such as the cornet, euphonium, horn or trumpet, and the wings of a bee when it is *'buzzing'.*

Musical Sounds and Noise

Not all sounds are musical. In general, we may say that for a musical sound to be produced, the vibrations of the source must be regular, that is, the frequency must remain constant for an appreciable interval of time thus producing some semblance of a note of definite pitch. Noise may be described as the result of confused or chaotic vibrations giving rise to indefiniteness of pitch. This is admittedly only a rough distinction. Are we to say that the clang of cymbals is not musical? Certainly it has no clearly marked pitch and yet cymbals may be employed most effectively in orchestration. Indeed, it is quite remarkable how the ear can pick out elements of definite pitch even in undoubted cases of noise as, for example, in the breaking of glass. This treatment of noise in terms of vibrations is essentially physical but there is also a psychological aspect. Noise may be regarded as any unwanted sound. To the dweller in a flat, the sound of the radio from the adjacent flat may be regarded as anything but musical despite the fact that an international virtuoso may be performing a great masterpiece!

Pitch and Frequency

In the above discussion it has been assumed that the reader understands what is meant by the pitch of a musical note. Pitch is one of the fundamental aural sensations enabling us to distinguish between notes as being 'high' or 'low' respectively—for example, the notes at the right-hand side of a piano would be called high in comparison with those at the left-hand side. We are however accustomed to make much more subtle comparisons of pitch than this in everyday speech. From the physical point of view pitch is determined by the frequency of the source of vibration. Quite apart from standards of pitch (with which we shall deal more fully later), we shall regard middle C on the piano as having a frequency of 256 vibrations, or cycles, per second (written 256 c/s.). This means that when we strike middle C, the strings associated with this note move to-and-fro 256 times per second. The bottom and top notes on the piano have frequencies of about 27 c/s and 4000 c/s respectively. It is only when we wish to describe the aural or musical properties of sounds that we need to use the term pitch. The effect of intensity on pitch will be considered later.

Transmission of Sound

Let us now consider what happens to the air in the neighbourhood of a vibrating metal strip. When the strip moves outwards it compresses the air in its immediate neighbourhood. On moving backwards to its furthest position on the other side of the central position, the compression originally produced moves outward by being communicated successively from layer to layer of air and is followed by a rarefaction due to the backward movement of the strip. Of course, the air on the outer side of the strip on the backward movement is now compressed so that when the strip moves forward again, a compression, followed by a rarefaction, will travel away from the strip. The elasticity of the air enables it to respond readily to these pressure changes. In this way, the continuous to-and-fro movement of the strip results in a series of compressions and rarefactions travelling outwards from the vibrating strip. No general mass movement of the air takes place for the strip of metal is relatively small in size and the air possesses considerable inertia.

When a sound passes through a cloud, the cloud does not move bodily forward. Instead, the particles of air in the cloud are moving forwards and backwards and the *phase* or relative positions of neighbouring particles give rise to local regions of compression and rarefaction. To achieve the distribution of compressions and rarefactions described above, the particles of air will be oscillating to-and-fro in the same line as that in which the compression with its relative rarefaction is travelling, each particle performing its motion a stage later than the particle immediately in front of it. If the behaviour of any individual particle is examined while the wave is passing, it will be seen to execute a simple to-and-fro movement, called *Simple Harmonic Motion*, (S.H.M.), along the line in which the sound is travelling. This is the same kind of movement as that described by a point on the piston of a steam engine while driving a fly wheel. Since the particle movements in air take place in the same line as that along which sound travels, sound is said to be propagated by *longitudinal* (or compressional) wave motion which thus distinguishes it from the transverse wave motion seen when waves travel along the surface of water.

The curve (a) in Fig. 3 (page 47) represents the variations in the pressure of the air that take place as a simple compressional wave such as that from a vibrating strip of steel moves forward. The graph resembles a transverse wave because we have shown by means of ordinates above the horizontal axis the amount of excess pressure in the different parts of the compressions. Similarly, below the axis we have shown the defect of pressure in the rarefactions. The compressions are regularly spaced and so are the rarefactions when the metal strip is vibrating uniformly. The distance from the centre of one compression to the centre of the next is called the *wave-length* and is usually designated by the Greek letter λ (*lambda*).

We may now deduce a simple but important relation between the frequency of vibration, the wave-length and the velocity of the wave. Clearly, the number of compressions originating from the vibrator each second will be equal to the number of to-and-fro movements which it makes, that is, frequency. If therefore, the frequency be denoted by n, then the total number of wave-lengths leaving the source each second will be n and the total *length* of these waves will be n multiplied by λ. In other words, the total length of waves passing a fixed point each second will be n multiplied by λ, that is, n λ which gives us the velocity of the waves. Denoting this velocity by V feet per second, we have therefore the following fundamental relationship,

$$V = n\lambda$$

As a simple example, if n is 275 c/s, V being 1,100 feet per second, the corresponding wave-length would be 1,100 divided by 275, namely four feet. In the same way the wave-length of the notes of a piano range in length from about 40 feet for the lowest notes to three inches for the highest.

It will have been seen from the above description that the air performs the important function of transmitting the sound energy from the vibrating source to the listener's ear. Sound may also be transmitted by liquids and solids. The essential point to notice is that a medium is essential between the source and the ear. In music and ordinary speech the medium is of course the air.

The Speed of Sound

At a cricket match it is readily noticed that an appreciable time elapses between the instants at which a 'hit' is seen and then heard by an observer in the pavilion. Owing to the enormous speed of light (186,000 miles per second), it may be assumed that the 'hit' is seen practically at the instant when the ball strikes the bat. The time lag in hearing the sound is due to the fact that sound travels comparatively slowly. Under ordinary conditions the speed of transmission of sound in air is about 1,100 feet per second, hence if the players are 100 yards from the pavilion, the time lag will be over a quarter of a second.

For the same reason, an organist playing at a detached console situated a considerable distance from the main body of the organ may notice a time lag between depressing a key and hearing the sound of the corresponding note. One section of the organ in the immense auditorium at Atlantic City, U.S.A., is 500 feet from the master console, hence the player hears the sounds from this section at an interval of about half a second late. Other examples will readily occur to the reader, thus a large choir may be in beat with the conductor but to a listener situated at one side, the time of the near and distant parts may not seem exact; again a long column of soldiers marching to a band at their head may not all be precisely in step for the sounds will reach the rear of the column appreciably late thereby creating an out of phase effect apparent to an observer at the side.

Direct methods of measuring the velocity of sound in air have been based on observations similar to the above, the time for sound to travel between two given points, say ten miles apart, being determined by means of a stop watch, due allowance being made for the effect of wind by timing the sound in each direction. The results of such work are now only of historical interest as more accurate laboratory methods are available.

Why Wind Instruments Go Out of Tune

From the musical point of view the *change* in value of the velocity of sound with changes in atmospheric condition is of more interest than the absolute value of the velocity, since variations in temperature and humidity alter the velocity and lead to corresponding variations in the tuning of some instruments, notably orchestral brass and woodwind, and flue organ pipes. Water vapour is lighter than air, consequently moist air is less dense than dry air and the velocity is increased by the presence of moisture. Remembering the relation $V = n\lambda$ derived above, we see that, if the velocity V increases, $n\lambda$ increases. Since λ remains practically constant, the effect of increase in velocity is mainly noticed through an increase in the value of n, that is, the pitch of the note rises. Similarly the velocity changes with temperature.

The exact relation between velocity and temperature is:—the velocity of sound in air is directly proportional to the square root of the absolute temperature. (Absolute temperature is obtained by adding 273 to the observed temperature expressed in degrees Centigrade, e.g. 10° Centigrade = (273 + 10°) Absolute.) The figure 273 is derived from the coefficient of expansion of air, namely, unit volume of air expands $\frac{1}{273}$ of its volume at 0° Centigrade for each degree rise in temperature. Taking the velocity of sound at 5° C. as *1089* feet per second, to find the velocity at 16° C. we have $\frac{V_{16}}{V_5} = \sqrt{\frac{273 + 16}{273 + 5}} = \sqrt{\frac{289}{278}}$ or $V_{16} = 1089 \times \sqrt{\frac{289}{278}} = 1119$ feet per second. Very roughly, the velocity increases by about two feet per second for each degree Centigrade rise in temperature or 1·1 feet per second for each degree Fahrenheit.

The following table gives some values of the velocity of sound for reference purposes:

Substance	Temperature	Velocity in feet per second	Velocity in metres per second
Air (dry)	0° C. (32° F.)	1088	332
Air (dry)	20° C. (68° F.)	1129	334
Hydrogen	0° C. (32° F.)	4165	1269
Oxygen	0° C. (32° F.)	1041	317
Water	0° C. (32° F.)	1315	401
Steel	20° C. (68° F.)	16,360	4990

Note that sounds of different pitch travel at the same velocity, otherwise concerted music as from an orchestra would not be possible, for the sounds from the different instruments would then reach the listener at different times, producing a chaotic effect.

Reflection of Sound

When a source of sound is vibrating, longitudinal or compressional waves spread out from the source through the air. If the air is homogeneous, that is, the temperature, humidity and other physical conditions are uniform, the waves will have the form of spheres of compression and rarefaction spreading outwards from the source as centre. When the waves meet an extended surface such as the wall of a room, they will be reflected provided that the irregularities of the surface are small compared with the wave-length of the waves, in other words, the surface is smooth. As we shall see later on, waves of short wavelength tend to be scattered at rough surfaces and the corresponding sound is said to be absorbed.

Echoes from walls and cliffs provide a well-known example of sound reflection. Sounds reaching a wall are turned back. If sounds are made at regular intervals, these echoes may be used to verify the value of the velocity of sound, thus, suppose a metronome be set to make its clicks every second; then if it be placed at a distance of about 550 feet from a fairly smooth wall, an observer at the same distance will notice that the echo of a click is received at the instant when the next click occurs, in other words the sound has travelled to the wall, where it is reflected and re-traversed its path making a total distance of twice 550 feet, that is, 1,100 feet covered in one second.

The spheres of compression are called *wave fronts* and the direction at right angles to the wave fronts along which the sound appears to travel are sometimes called *rays* by analogy with the phenomenon of light. There is also a law of reflection of sound corresponding to that for the reflection of light from a mirror; namely, the angle of reflection is equal to the angle of incidence, the angles being measured between the respective rays and the normal (which is at right angles) to the surface at the point of incidence. Obviously if the sound is incident at right angles to the surface it will be reflected back along the same path.

The action of a whispering gallery as in St. Paul's Cathedral, London, is easily explained in terms of the reflection of sound. A sound is reflected successively with little loss from the inside to the outside wall of the circular corridor and is so transmitted round the dome and may be picked up at any point. The reader will readily see why a short sharp sound made in front of a flight of steps or a row of equally spaced palings returns as a musical tone by considering the successive reflections from the uniformly spaced individual steps or palings respectively.

Refraction of Sound

When sound waves pass from one medium to another of greater density, e.g. from air to carbon dioxide, they are slowed down. The phenomenon is analogous to what happens when light passes from air into glass. It is thus possible to produce an acoustic lens which will change the direction of sound waves exactly as happens when light passes through a glass lens. This may be done by using a large toy balloon filled with carbon dioxide to focus the sound waves from a ticking watch.

Refraction effects often occur in the atmosphere, thus warm air being less dense than cold air transmits sound with a greater velocity. In the day time when the earth is warm the air near the ground is warmer and therefore less dense than that higher up. Sound travelling more quickly near the ground than higher up results in the sound waves becoming deviated upwards and are therefore lost. The reverse occurs at night for which reason it is sometimes said that sounds carry better at night.

Diffraction of Sound

It is a well-known fact that sound waves can bend round corners. This phenomenon is called diffraction. It occurs also with light waves, but owing to the excessively small wave-length of light waves (of the order of 1/50,000 of an inch), the phenomena can only be studied and observed in special cases. With sound, however, the wave-lengths concerned are of considerable magnitude, often several feet long, so that the bending is easily noticed. If, however, the obstacle is of vast size compared with the sound waves, it may prove to be an effective barrier and an *acoustic shadow* is produced. As a rule however some sound energy does reach the side of the obstacle remote from the sound and the shadow is therefore only partial.

Interference or Superposition of Sound Waves

The individual air particles oscillate to-and-fro in the line along which a sound is travelling. If two waves are caused to travel along the same line at the same time, each particle will experience two simultaneously acting forces tending to cause it to be displaced. The varied possibilities of the motion are easily imagined. For example, consider a particle acted on at a given instant due to one of the two wave motions so that it tends to move in one direction, while the other wave motion tends to cause it to move equally in the opposite direction. Clearly the particle cannot respond to the two forces at the same time and it will therefore remain at rest.

If one of the forces is slightly less than the other then the particle will be displaced in the direction of action of the larger force by an amount determined by the difference between the two forces. In the same way it can be seen that when the forces acting on an air particle by the two waves simultaneously tend in the same direction, the particle will move much more vigorously than when one wave only is being transmitted through the medium. In the latter case the two waves are said to be in phase, that is, the crests and troughs of the pressure curve from one set coincide with the crests and troughs from the other set and the effect in the air is greatly intensified; in other words the resultant sound will become louder. When the waves are out of phase, the motion of each air particle will be diminished by an amount determined by the degree of 'out-of-phaseness', with a corresponding reduction in the loudness of the sound produced, indeed, two sets of waves of the same wave-length and amplitude completely out-of-phase would so neutralise each other's effect that no sound would result. The reader can easily see this by drawing the pressure curve of a wave and superimposing upon it another wave of the same wave-length and amplitude but making the troughs of the latter correspond to crests of the former from which it will appear that the two waves neutralise each other, being completely out-of-phase. This is called destructive interference.

Interference may easily be demonstrated with an ordinary tuning fork. On rotating the fork near the ear while it is vibrating, the sound will appear to wax and wane four times for each complete rotation, as a result of the interference between the compressions and rarefactions arising from the alternative movements outwards and inwards of the prongs.

Organ builders are well acquainted with the phenomenon of interference and it is for this reason that they avoid placing pipes of the same pitch close together on the soundboards of an organ. Such pipes of course emit waves of the same wave-length under conditions favouring destructive interference. Out of phaseness of the sets of waves from the pipes may readily become established so that the condensations emitted by one pipe neutralise rarefactions due to its neighbour.

Stationary or Standing Waves

An interesting and important case of the superposition of sound waves in air occurs when sound is reflected from a wall along its original line of transmission. A little consideration will show that owing to the rigid character of the wall, the air particles in the neighbourhood of the wall must necessarily be reversed in motion when reflection of an on-coming wave takes place and the wave is said to be reflected with change of phase.

We have now to consider the superposition of two sets of

waves in the same line, namely the on-coming waves and the reflected waves. The particles in the condensations of the on-coming wave are travelling in the same direction as those of the rarefactions in the reflected wave hence condensations of one set of waves meet rarefactions in the other; reinforcement occurs. Similarly, incident condensations superimposed on reflected rarefactions give neutralisation of air movements. In this way, a stationary state arises such that at some points called *nodes* the air is always at rest, while in the spaces between these, called *antinodes*, there exists a permanent condition of pulsating movement. A compression in the on-coming wave is reflected as a compression, hence we have a node or point of no movement of air particles at the wall. We should, of course, expect from general considerations that the layer of air in contact with the wall would be at rest. At equally spaced intervals of half a wave-length we have other nodes and between these the antinodes or *loops* as they are sometimes called in which vigorous pulsations are taking place. There is no progressive movement of the waves, hence the description *stationary* or *standing waves*.

Stationary waves may often be observed in a church if a low-pitched note is sounded on the organ. Points of silence (nodes) will be detected due to the interaction of the forward wave and that reflected from a wall. A few feet away from these points the sound may be quite intense. Thus if the waves have a frequency of 32 c/s the wave-length will be about 34 feet and the distance between the nodes 17 feet. On moving say, eight feet from a node, a loud sound will be heard. In the same way a high-pitched whistle sounding in an ordinary room will give rise to stationary waves. In this case the waves are of short wave-length—a matter of a few inches—and a slight movement only of the head will enable one to pass from a loop to a node. It is usually best to cover one ear in making the observation.

Chladni's Figures

A beautiful method of demonstrating stationary waves visually occurs in the *transverse* vibration of plates. For the purpose a thin plate of metal about ten inches square is mounted horizontally by means of a support in the middle. A thin layer of sand is sprinkled on the plate and the plate is caused to vibrate by bowing with a 'cello bow at suitable points along the edge. Different notes may be produced according to the point of bowing (which will obviously be a loop) and the point or points at which the motion is damped by touching it with the fingers— these are of course nodes. While the plate is vibrating, transverse waves travel across it and are reflected from the edges in consequence of which stationary waves are set up by the interaction of the two sets. The points of 'no motion' link up to form nodal lines along which the sand collects after being shaken from the loops. The nodal lines often constitute quite complicated patterns known as Chladni's figures according to the notes generated.

Figure 1 illustrates the kind of result obtained. Plates of shapes other than the square may obviously be investigated. The modes of vibration of telephone diaphragms may also be studied in this way and attempts have been made to use these figures in the investigation of the vibrations of the plates of a violin. Organ tuners occasionally find Chladni's figures in the dust lying on the tuning caps of certain organ pipes. By using a forked tube with the double limbs directed respectively over alternate or adjacent antinodal areas of Chladni's figures, and listening carefully at the other end, the out-of-phase motion of the different parts of the plate may be observed, thus verifying

that the figures arise from the interaction of different sets
of waves crossing the plate.

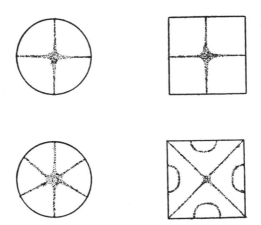

Fig. 1. Examples of Chladni's sand figures for square and circular
plates.

Beats

An important example of interference between two sets
of sound waves occurs when the sources differ only
slightly in frequency, or in other words, the waves from
one source are nearly equal to those from the other
source. It should not be difficult to see that if the two sets
of waves start off in phase—say the compressions from
one coincide with the compressions from the other thus
producing a loud sound—owing to the difference in wave-
length the waves will gradually become out of step and
one set will temporarily work to some extent in opposition
to the other set, the resulting sound being much weaker.
They will then tend to become in step again and so on.
Hence the effect is that the resultant sound from the two
sources alternately waxes and wanes in intensity, giving
rise to a pulsating or beating effect.

The number of *beats* made each second is equal to the difference in the frequencies of the two sources. Thus, two sources of frequencies 384 c/s and 380 c/s will give rise to four beats per second, for the source of higher frequency will obviously gain (384 − 380) vibrations per second over the lower one. This effect is easily observed. Of two forks in unison the note from one may be lowered slightly by fastening a piece of wire round the end of one of its prongs. By sliding the wire along the prong, the number of beats made with the second fork may be adjusted to any desired degree.

Beats have a wide application in music. The tuning of pianos and organs to equal temperament can only be done through a careful consideration of the beats between certain special intervals used in 'laying the bearings' while beats must be eliminated between the strings common to each note of the piano. The peculiar wavy effect of beats is turned to advantage in the *céleste* stop of the organ in which two ranks of small scaled string toned stops are purposely left slightly out of tune so that the wavy effect may suggest the shimmering of orchestral string tone. Beats also figure significantly in the theory of consonance and dissonance. This will be discussed more fully when we consider the phenomena of sum and difference tones (p. 64).

Forced Vibrations and Resonance

A vibrating tuning fork held in the hand emits so feeble a sound that it must be placed close to the ear to be heard. However, by standing its shank in contact with an extended surface such as a tabletop, the sound appears to be augmented considerably. The surface of the table has been *forced* into vibration by the vibrating fork and so a greater mass of air is affected than when the prongs vibrate alone. If the forced vibrations in the table have the same frequency as those of the fork, specially great enhancement of the sound takes place and the phenomenon of *resonance* occurs.

Resonance is one of the most commonly occurring phenomena in vibratory motion and as we shall see has numerous applications in practical music. In a motor car, for example, loosely fitting doors or windows may pick up the vibrations of the engine when their frequencies of vibration are the same and a 'rattle' is the result. There is the often quoted mechanical example of the necessity for soldiers marching over a swing bridge to break step in case the frequency of the marching shall be the same as that of the natural vibrations of the structure, in which event the amplitude of the vibrations built up in the bridge by resonance might cause a breakdown of the supports. An accident of this kind is reported as having occurred at Broughton, Manchester, in 1831, when a rifle corps of 80 soldiers were precipitated into a river through the collapse of a suspension bridge. Many acoustical illustrations of resonance may be cited, e.g. air in a bottle of suitable volume will reinforce the note of a tuning fork held in the mouth of the bottle; two strings tuned to unison suitably mounted on a soundboard will pick up each other's vibrations when one only is excited externally.

Though resonance is part of the general theory of vibrations, it is convenient from the acoustical point of view to state the *principle of resonance* as follows: If two sources of sound are tuned to unison and one of them is excited by external means, the second source will pick up the vibrations from the first by 'sympathy' or resonance without external stimulation. Illustrations of acoustical resonance will be noted in later references to musical instruments.

III

PITCH AND THE MUSICAL SCALE

'Order and proportion in sounds makes music'
Sir Isaac Newton

The Characteristics of Musical Sounds

Musical sounds possess three properties, namely (1) pitch, (2) loudness, and (3) quality, which are so well defined that until recent years it was customary among physicists never to regard them otherwise than as quite separate characteristics. Further studies, largely resulting from development in the psychology of hearing, have shown that we cannot ignore some degree of interrelatedness between them, for example, a marked increase in the loudness of a tone may under some circumstances produce a change in its pitch. Relatedness of this kind is of obvious importance to the musical listener.

We have already stressed that the pitch of a note is determined by the frequency of vibration of the source. Similarly, loudness is determined by the intensity of the vibration of the source. The quality, or timbre, is that property which distinguishes notes of the same pitch when sounded by various instruments, thus 'middle C' sounded on the piano is readily distinguished from the note of the same pitch sounded on the violin or flute. The reason for this will be given iater.

Frequency and its Measurement

The pitch of a note is determined by the number of vibrations made by the source per second. This number

33

is too big for the impulses given to the air to be counted separately, so that special devices must be arranged for the purpose. In the siren a circular disc of metal has a number of small holes drilled through it at equal distances apart in a circle concentric with the edge of the disc. The disc is rotated by suitable means while a jet of air plays through the circle of holes. In this way a number of regular puffs of air, producing impulses that give rise to compressional waves, pass through the disc, hence at a suitable steady speed of rotation a musical note is produced. If there are 24 holes in the circle and the disc is making 960 revolutions per minute, or 16 per second, the frequency of the resulting note will be $24 \times 16 = 384$ c/s, which is the G above middle C on the piano.

This provides a method of determining the pitch of any note, for all that is necessary is to adjust the speed of the disc so that its note is in unison with that whose frequency is to be measured and calculate as above. The method is only approximate even when an automatic counting mechanism is attached to the disc but it does bring out clearly the dependence of pitch on frequency. In much the same way a rotating toothed wheel may be employed. A card is placed against the teeth. The flicking of the card as each tooth passes provides the impulses for the compressional waves.

Another method of frequency determination involves the actual measurement of the length of the transverse waves traced on a suitable surface by the vibrating source while either the source or the surface moves at a known rate e.g. if the source is a tuning fork, a very fine style is attached to one of the prongs by means of a piece of soft wax. While the fork is vibrating, a smoked glass plate carried on a trolley is drawn at a known uniform speed under the fork so that the style makes a wavy trace on the plate. From the speed of movement of the trolley the time taken for a number of complete wave-lengths to be traced may be found from which the frequency may be calculated. The falling plate experiment described in text-books of physics is a variant of this method. Another variant is to allow the style on the tuning fork to make its wavy trace on a sheet of card mounted on a gramophone turntable and obtain the timing from the speed of rotation.

More accurate methods of determining frequency involve the use of a sonometer or a resonance tube assuming the laws of vibrating strings and columns of air respectively. For details, text-books of physics should be consulted.

Electrically Driven Tuning Fork

For accurate acoustic work especially in the psychological laboratory it is necessary to have sources of sound of constant frequency. Tuning forks having their vibrations maintained at constant speed by electrical methods have been designed for the purpose. In one such fork the prongs are driven by an electro-magnetic action similar to that of an ordinary electric bell. In his important work on the extent to which the ear can discriminate between sounds of slightly different pitch Seashore used electrically driven forks accurate to one thousandth of a vibration.

Standards of Pitch

The pitch at which music is performed has varied very considerably at different periods. According to Fellowes, in Tudor times there were actually three different standards in use, namely, that of domestic keyboard instruments which was a tone-and-a-half below that of today, that of secular vocal music—about the same as today, and that of church music—about a tone higher than today. Handel's tuning fork was about half a tone lower than today's pitch. In general the standard of pitch has tended to rise with the development of instrumental music, for instruments sound more brilliant at high pitches and the bounds of discretion in this respect have tended to be ignored. Clearly, where voices have to be accompanied by instruments, some reasonable standard must be adopted if absurd feats of transposition during performance are to be avoided. Care should of course be taken to endeavour to secure in performance a close approximation to the composer's intentions for the musical effect is dependent upon the pitch used.

Nomenclature for Pitch

For the identification of the various octaves used in practical music, we shall use the following nomenclature, which is practically that adopted by organ builders, making middle C on the piano keyboard the reference point. CCCC represents the note from an open organ pipe 32 feet long; CCC, that from a 16 foot pipe; CC, that from an eight foot pipe; etc. Bottom C on the piano keyboard will be represented by CCC and top C (four octaves above middle C) by C^4, the various octaves being CCC—CC; CC—C; C—Mid. C; Mid. C—C^1; C^1—C^2; C^2—C^3; C^3—C^4 ('top C' on a modern pianoforte).

At last there seems an end to the diverse standards of pitch in practical music. An International Conference on pitch held in London in May, 1939 agreed that the frequency for the standard of orchestral pitch should be A (second space treble clef) equal to 440 c/s. As already noted, the pitch of many orchestral instruments rises with rise in temperature so that it is necessary to indicate a temperature at which this frequency shall hold. The British Standards Institution specifies a temperature of 20° C. or 68° F.

It only remains to add that for convenience in calculation, scientists usually assume middle C on the piano =

256 c/s on account of its being a convenient multiple of two. (According to the International Standard, 'middle C' is 261·6 c/s.) Actually the difference is of no material significance for usually we are concerned with the ratios between frequencies.

Musical Intervals

Any two musical sounds form an interval with each other whether played together or in sequence. An interval is represented numerically by dividing the frequency of the upper note by that of the lower and the result may be reduced to its lowest terms by cancelling common factors in the numerator and denominator. Thus two notes having the frequencies 256 c/s and 384 c/s respectively would form an interval represented by the fraction $\frac{384}{256}$ which, by cancelling common factors, reduces to the simple relation $\frac{3}{2}$. This is the perfect fifth. Similarly, notes whose frequencies are related by the ratio $\frac{2}{1}$ are an octave apart. The perfect fourth is represented by $\frac{4}{3}$ and no matter in which octave the perfect fourth occurs, the frequencies of the corresponding notes will always reduce to the ratio $\frac{4}{3}$.

To add together two intervals, it is necessary to multiply together their corresponding frequency ratios, for example, the interval C to E (a major third $= \frac{5}{4}$) plus the interval E to G (a minor third $= \frac{6}{5}$) gives the interval C to G, a perfect fifth, that is $\frac{5}{4} \times \frac{6}{5} = \frac{6}{4} = \frac{3}{2}$ (as mentioned above).

(CAUTION: Though treatises on the theory of music often define an interval as the *difference* in pitch between two notes, we must *never* attempt to express an interval numerically by subtracting one frequency from another. An interval is essentially a *relation* between two notes which is true in whatever octave of the musical range it may occur; the mathematical method of expressing a

Oct	5th	4th	M3	m3	M2	m2	M6	m6
$\frac{2}{1}$	$\frac{3}{2}$	$\frac{4}{3}$	$\frac{5}{4}$	$\frac{6}{5}$	$\frac{9}{8}$ or $\frac{10}{9}$	$\frac{16}{15}$	$\frac{5}{3}$	$\frac{12}{5}$

Major Triad 4:5:6

relation is by means of a *ratio* between the constituent numbers, which is therefore independent of the absolute values of individual frequencies. Students often fall into error through overlooking this basic fact.)

The Musical Scale and Equal Temperament

It is not possible to discuss intervals satisfactorily without making some reference to the mental effect of pairs of notes when sounded together. The notes of some intervals, for example the octave, perfect fifth and perfect fourth, seem to merge or blend so well when sounded together that they are described as consonant; other combinations have a rough effect by comparison. We shall suggest a reason for this later on. It is rather striking that the consonant intervals are in general represented by simple numerical ratios; thus the octave, the most consonant interval of all, has the ratio 2/1 and the next most consonant interval, the perfect fifth, the ratio 3/2. The tritone fourth between F and B, known in olden days as *diabolus in musica* because of its uncouthness, is represented by the complex ratio 45/32.

A musical scale is a series of notes arranged in order of pitch according to some prescribed system. It is therefore easily seen that musicians have almost an unlimited variety of possible scales at their disposal. One system arranges the notes so that the interval relations in the series are those of the more consonant intervals, that is to say, they are represented by simple numerical ratios. This scale is variously called the natural, ideal, just or pure diatonic scale. Representing the various degrees of this scale by Roman numerals, the frequencies of the constituent notes will always be related as shown below:

Scale degree	I	II	III	IV	V	VI	VII	VIII
Relative frequency number	24	27	30	32	36	40	45	48

Thus, the interval between the first and eighth degrees is $48/24 = 2/1$, the octave; between the first and fifth degrees, $36/24 = 3/2$, the perfect fifth; between the first and fourth degrees, $32/24 = 4/3$, the perfect fourth; between the fourth and eighth degrees, $48/32 = 3/2$, the perfect fifth; etc.

A scale on this system starting from middle C = 256 c/s would proceed as follows:

C	D	E	F	G	A	B	C (octave).
256	288	320	341·3	384	426·6	480	512 c/s

In the same way a scale could be constructed beginning on any other note; the only condition to be observed would be that the frequency ratio of any pair of notes must reduce to the relative frequency numbers shown against corresponding Roman numerals above. The major triad, C — E — G, is given by the ratios 24: 30: 36 or 4: 5: 6.

The successive intervals in the natural scale are as follows:

I	II	III	IV	V	VI	VII	VIII
24	27	30	32	36	40	45	48

Interval

$$9/8 \quad 10/9 \quad 16/15 \quad 9/8 \quad 10/9 \quad 9/8 \quad 16/15$$
$$= 1·125 = 1·111 = 1·067 = 1·125 = 1·111 = 1·125 = 1·067$$

The interval $9/8$ is a major tone, $10/9$ a minor tone and $16/15$ a limma. There are thus two kinds of whole tone $9/8$ and $10/9$; the limma corresponds to a semi-tone. Note that two limmas added together are not equal to either a major tone or minor tone, thus $1·067 \times 1·067 = 1·138$ whereas the major tone is $1·125$ and the minor tone $1·111$.

The difference between the major and minor tones namely $\frac{9}{8} \times \frac{9}{10} = \frac{81}{80}$ is called the comma of Didymus. The difference between the minor tone and the limma is called the diesis and equals $\frac{10}{9} \times \frac{15}{16} = \frac{25}{24}$.

A number of natural scales formed on different keynotes by making the intervals from each keynote as indicated above lead to the situation that the same note on different scales appears to have different frequencies according to the particular scale from which it has been derived, for example, the note A has a frequency of 426·6 c/s when derived from the keynote C = 256 c/s but when the keynote is D = 288 c/s it has the frequency 432 c/s. It is clear therefore that modulation from one key to another on a piano tuned to the natural scale would be intolerable from the musical standpoint.

Several systems of tuning keyboard instruments have been tried at various times in order to overcome this disadvantage of the natural scale, notably the method of mean tone tuning of the period of Bach and Handel which aimed at equalising the major and minor tones and relating them to the limma by making the major thirds fairly accurate. This and other methods have however at long last given way to the system of *equal temperament* which is universal today. In this, the octave is divided into twelve equal semitones. From the rule for the addition of intervals given above the vibration ratio for the equal tempered semitone may be easily calculated. Since there are 12 semitones in the octave, if S denote the interval ratio of a semitone, then S raised to the power of 12, that is, S^{12}, is equal to the numerical ratio for the octave, namely 2/1, so that $S^{12} = 2/1$, whence S is the twelfth-root of two, namely 1·059. A tone (that is, two semitones) is therefore 1·059 x 1·059 = 1·121 which may be compared with the major tone (= 1·125) and the minor tone (= 1·111) of the natural scale.

We now give for reference purposes the frequency of each note in an octave of the equal tempered scale derived by steps of a semitone from the International Standard A (treble clef) = 440 c/s.

Note	*Frequency*
C_1 (Middle C on the piano)	261·6 c/s
C_1 Sharp = D_1 flat	277·2 c/s
D_1	293·7 c/s
D_1 Sharp = E_1 flat	311·1 c/s
E_1	329·6 c/s
F_1	349·2 c/s *261.9*
F_1 Sharp = G_1 flat	370·0 c/s
G_1	392·0 c/s *261.3*
G_1 Sharp = A_1 flat	415·3 c/s
A_1 (International Standard)	440 c/s
A_1 Sharp = B_1 flat	466·2 c/s
B_1	493·9 c/s
C_2 (Octave of mid. C on the piano)	523·2 c/s

From the mode of its derivation, the equal tempered scale is obviously one of compromise. The chromatic notes such as C sharp and D flat, which according to tuning on the natural scale are separate notes, are now represented by one key only on the piano keyboard. Then again even the fundamental intervals, the perfect fifth or the perfect fourth are no longer true, the former being slightly flat and the latter slightly sharp. Only the octave is perfect. Tuning a keyboard instrument to equal temperament is a task therefore demanding considerable skill and experience. Most methods of tuning involve tuning the fourths and fifths perfect and then sharpening and flattening them as necessary by listening to the beats produced. For details one of the many practical manuals should be consulted.

To the keyboard player, equal temperament permits freedom to modulate at will among the various keys. As a system of tuning it was favoured by no less a musician than J. S. Bach whose first collection of preludes and fugues in all the keys, *Das Wohltemperirtes Clavier*, dates from 1722. A second similar book was issued in 1744. Mean-tone tuning was only good for modulation into a few keys fairly closely related to the home key; further afield a harshness (called the wolf) produced the clash of out-of-tune intervals, greatly limiting the scope of the music. Even so equal temperament came into general use only slowly. Some important English organs used mean-tone tuning as late as 1880.

Enharmonic organs in which all notes of the scale including the chromatic C sharp, D flat etc., are tuned exact according to the natural scale have been constructed but are little more than scientific curiosities being very complicated to play. Several examples may be inspected at the Science Museum, South Kensington, London.

IV

COLOUR IN MUSIC

'A series of qualities of tone are analysed in respect to their harmonic upper partial tones, and it results that these upper partial tones are not, as was hitherto thought, isolated phenomena of small importance, but that, with very few exceptions, they determine the qualities of tone of almost all instruments, and are of the greatest importance for those qualities of tone which are best adapted for musical purposes.'

Helmholtz

Overtones

The sounds of the respective instruments of the orchestra are readily distinguished from one another, thus a violin and a cornet playing a note of the same pitch and loudness sound quite different, indeed, it is such differences that constitute the whole *raison d'être* of the orchestra. Each instrument is said to possess its own peculiar *tone quality,* or *timbre.* The corresponding German term is *Klangfarbe*—tone colour—which expresses very aptly that the tonal differences of the various instruments are to the musician what the colours in his palette are to the painter. No other acoustical topic is of more importance in practical music than that of the study of the qualities of tones; orchestration—the art of combining tone qualities—has derived, and continues to derive, considerable impetus from physical investigations on the nature of quality.

The basic fact in the explanation of tone quality is that tones are rarely simple in structure. The notes of the violin, piano, cornet, oboe, etc., consist of a fundamental

43

sound whose pitch gives the name to the note, together with a number of higher pitched sounds, called *overtones*, whose frequencies are related quite simply to those of the fundamental but whose intensities vary according to the instrument used for producing them. Taking the most general case (represented in practice by a vibrating column of air in a fairly wide pipe or by a long, very flexible stretched string), we have to imagine musical tones as consisting of a fundamental of a certain frequency sounding together with a number of overtones of frequencies twice, three times, four times etc. . . the frequency of the fundamental. Usually the overtones decrease gradually in intensity the higher the frequency but this is not necessarily so as much depends on the manner in which the sounds are being produced. Any change in the intensity of the overtones, including the case when some of them are of zero intensity (for example in a stopped organ pipe, or a clarinet) will produce changes in quality as appreciated by the listener.

The sequence of fundamental and overtones gives the *harmonic series;* if n c/s is the frequency of the fundamental, then the most general form of the harmonic series will be n, $2n$, $3n$, $4n$, $5n$, etc . . . Expressing this in musical intervals we therefore have *fundamental* (n), *octave* ($2n$), *twelfth* ($3n$), *fifteenth* ($4n$), *seventeenth* ($5n$), *nineteenth* ($6n$), etc.

Figure 2 gives in musical notation the lower members of the harmonic series for the note CC, as obtained for example from an open organ pipe of speaking length about 8 ft (see p. 36) assuming the frequency 64 c/s for the fundamental. Organists will recognise the traditional names *tierce* and *larigot* for the seventeenth and nineteenth as stops so named were often used in old organs to intensify these particular overtones in the ensembles of the instrument and for synthesising new tones.

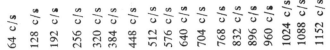

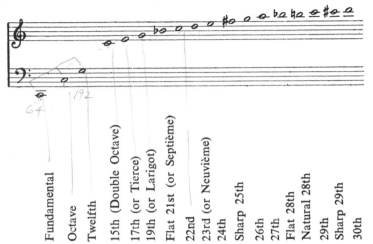

Fig. 2. The first seventeen overtones of the fundamental note C = 64 c/s in musical notation. The frequencies are untempered.

Attention must be drawn to some variance in the nomenclature of overtones. That given above is commonly used by musicians and is both descriptive and adequate to its purpose. Physicists however usually describe the fundamental or generating tone as the first harmonic or first partial tone, the octave as the second harmonic or second partial tone and so on.

Notice that the overtones sound simultaneously with the fundamental, in other words, each note of a musical instrument is a complex of sounds. The aural effect of the complex is dependent on the relative intensities of the overtone content. The presence of the lower pitched overtones may sometimes be detected by careful listening. Helmholtz employed special resonators to aid the ear. These consisted of metal spheres of graded volume to respond to particular overtones. An aperture for the sound to enter the resonator was provided and another on the opposite side at which the ear was placed. The presence of the corresponding overtones in a note would be detected by its reinforcement through the sympathetic vibration of the air in the resonator. When we deal with the instruments of the orchestra we shall find that in many of them, playing technique involves a detailed knowledge of, and is conditioned by, overtone development.

Graphical Representation of Quality

We have already described (p. 19) how a simple compressional wave may be represented by a curve showing the fluctuations in pressure that take place in the air as the wave advances. In view of what has been said above regarding the complexity of the notes of musical instruments we can readily see that when a note is sounded, a large number of compressional waves differing from each other in wave-length and amplitude are being emitted at the same time, each making its own demand of air movement. Since individual air particles cannot move in several directions at the same time, it is clear that the movement of any particular particle will be the resultant of all the demands made on it by the several constituent waves.

It is now possible to obtain photographs of the wave forms of musical tones direct from the sounding instrument using a cathode ray oscillograph. The sound when received by a microphone gives rise to alternating electric potentials which in turn act upon a narrow stream of cathode rays in a suitable vacuum tube causing corresponding displacements of the rays to produce tracks on a fluorescent screen, similar to the curves of Figure 3. The tracks may be photographed directly. Of course the air particles do not move in tracks such as these. As already explained, these transverse curves are only a convenient way of presenting graphically the *changes in pressure* that take place as the sound waves advance through the air.

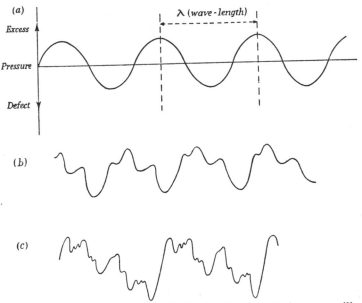

Fig. 3. Specimen wave curves obtained with a cathode ray oscillo-graph. (a) Tuning fork; (b) Flute; (c) Pianoforte.

Acoustic Spectra

The above explanation of the quality of musical sounds implies that any musical tone may be specified by stating the frequencies of its fundamental and associated over-tones together with the intensity of each constituent. When represented in a diagram these give rise to an *acoustic spectrum,* analogous to the optical spectrum obtained from the decomposition of light into its constituent wave-lengths. Figure 4 illustrates the frequencies of the con-stituents of the G string of a violin and their relative intensities.

The Helmholtz resonators are not adequate for the close analysis required in determining acoustic spectra and electrical methods are now usually employed in which readily measureable electric currents are produced corresponding to the overtone constituents of sounds received by the attached microphone. Careful investigation shows that, except possibly for very loud sounds, quality is independent of phase of vibration and that therefore the

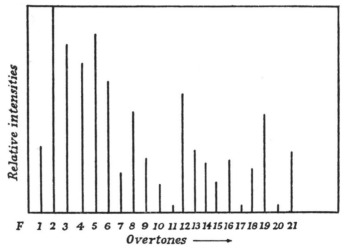

Fig. 4. Acoustic spectrum giving the overtone analysis of the G string of a violin.

acoustic spectrum, depending as it does on frequencies of intensity only, is an adequate specification of musical tone.

Synthesis of Tones

Analysis might be expected to imply synthesis. Helmholtz, who was the first to demonstrate successfully the analysis of tones into fundamental and overtones, achieved considerable success in synthesising tones from electrically driven tuning forks whose notes may be taken

to be almost devoid of overtones. By sounding simultaneously several forks of pitches according to the harmonic series and varying their relative intensities he was
able to reproduce a variety of orchestral tones. On organs
provided with certain ranks of pipes of high pitch it is
possible to combine the stops in such a way as to produce
a close semblance of clarinet or other reed tone. Synthesis
is also the basis of several forms of electrotonic organ.
Orchestration and organ registration are both arts that
depend upon the skill in synthesising tones.

Acoustical analysis and synthesis as just described are
really special cases of the application of a general principle
applicable to all cases of wave motion discovered by the
French engineer Fourier, according to which any wave
form may be analysed into a number of simple harmonic
constituents, thus, the wave form showing the rise and
fall of the River Thames at London Bridge over a period
of time is a very complicated curve but by Fourier's
principle it may be analysed into a number of simple
harmonic constituents, the study of which clearly reveals
the many factors which go towards determining the
changes in water level e.g. the variations in the rainfall on
the Cotswold Hills, the phases of the moon, etc.

Formants and Transients

Recent developments in acoustical engineering, while
serving to confirm the overtone theory of quality, have
also revealed that two other factors having a physical basis
enter into the aesthetic appreciation of the tone quality of
musical instruments, namely, (1) a contribution made by
parts of the instrument other than the main source of
vibrations and (2) the mode in which the tone builds up.
To illustrate (1) we may refer to the violin in which the
prime generators are the strings. The overtone theory is
quite adequate to deal with their tone production. How-

ever, superimposed on this is a modification of tone due to resonance responses from the body of the violin itself. Similarly, in an organ pipe or other wind instrument, the material of the body will give rise to a modification of the tone from the enclosed air column. The full significance of these modifying factors, called *formants,* is scarcely yet appreciated. They are mentioned here because a false impression has often been evident that seemed to imply a breakdown in the overtone theory.

formants

In regard to (2) it is now realised that the particular way in which the tone of an instrument begins is musically significant e.g. the characteristic 'piff' of the flute or the 'scratch' of the bow on the violin string. These initial tonal characteristics are named *transients.* Tonal deficiencies in synthetic electrotonic organs may often be traced back to the lack of formants and transients in the tone. Whether or not they may be simulated is often rather a matter of expense than of physical difficulty.

transients

Doppler Effect

This is an interesting acoustic effect which we note in passing. It is concerned with a change of pitch due to the relative motion of the source and the listener when the source is sounding. An observer standing on the platform of a railway station while an express train is travelling through notices a drop in pitch of the whistle of the engine as the train passes him. Actually the pitch of the whistle sounds higher than its normal pitch when the train is approaching and lower than its normal pitch when the train is receding, hence the sudden change as noticed by the observer. This is called the Doppler effect. It may easily be explained by the fact that when the whistle is approaching the observer the air compressions emitted are being crowded together due to the motion of the train which is so to speak trying to overtake the compressions, and the wave-length of the note of the whistle is thus apparently reduced with consequent increase in pitch (since $V = n\lambda$ and V may be regarded as constant for this purpose). Similarly, when the whistle is receding from the observer the wave-lengths appear to be 'lengthened' corresponding to a fall in pitch.

If V ft/sec is the velocity of sound, v ft/sec. the velocity of the train and n the frequency of the whistle, then in one second a compression from the whistle will have travelled a distance V feet while the train will have travelled v feet and the whistle will have emitted n compressions, hence the total length of the waves corresponding to these n compressions will now occupy only $V - v$ feet. So the new wave length will be $\frac{V-v}{n}$. This is the wavelength of the whistle as it appears to an observer at rest towards whom the train is approaching.

Since the velocity of sound is equal to frequency multiplied by wave-length, then the new frequency is obtained by dividing the velocity of sound by the new wave-length, hence n_1, the new frequency $= V \frac{V-v}{n}$. By the same argument it is easily seen that when the train is receding from the observer, the apparent frequency n_2 to the observer, will be given by $V \frac{V+v}{n}$.

The interval through which the note of the whistle appears to drop as the train passes the observer is thus given by

$$\frac{n_1}{n_2} = \frac{V+v}{V-v}$$

As an example, if the frequency of the whistle of an engine is 768 c/s and it is approaching an observer at rest with a speed of 60 miles/hour (or 88ft/sec), assuming the velocity of sound to be 1100 ft/sec, its apparent frequency will be

$$768 \times \frac{1100}{1100-88} = 768 \times \frac{1100}{1012} = 835 \text{ c/s}$$

that is the pitch of the note will have risen nearly a whole tone.

If now the train passes and recedes from the observer, the pitch will fall through the interval

$$\frac{1100+88}{1100-88} = \frac{1188}{1012} = 1 \cdot 174$$

that is about a whole tone.

Many examples of the Doppler effect will be found in every-day life in which moving sources of sound occur. The effect may be readily demonstrated by swinging a high pitched tuning fork in a circle. The concertina player at the music hall adds a wavy effect to his playing by swinging his instrument in a circle whose plane is directed towards the audience.

V

TONE PRODUCTION AND REPRODUCTION

'He despises nothing that bears the name of tone, sound, clang; he makes use of unbraced kettledrums, harps, muted horns, English horns and even bells.'

Schumann on *Berlioz*

Musical Instruments

Musical instruments are of course the external means by which musical sounds are produced by performers; they must therefore consist of a suitable source of vibration together with some means by which the player may control the intensity and pitch of the resulting sounds. As a rule the quality of these sounds is already determined by the instrument maker though in a few cases such as string and brass instruments a slight perceptible change in quality may be introduced through the way in which the player 'produces' his tone.

The sounds of the string family—violin, viola, violoncello, double bass—originate from the vibrations of stretched strings. The pitch of the notes produced depends on two factors, namely, (a) the length of the vibrating segment and (b) the tension of the corresponding string according to well established experimental laws:—(1) the *Law of Pythagoras* that, if all other factors remain constant, the frequency of the note from a stretched string is inversely proportional to the length of the vibrating segment; (2) the *Law of Mersenne* that, if all other factors remain constant, the frequency of the note from a

53

stretched string varies as the square root of the tension (for example, if the frequency is doubled, the tension will be quadrupled).

Use is made of the latter law in tuning string instruments by tightening or slackening the pegs. According to the former law, the performer produces notes of various pitches by pressing the strings firmly on the finger board, thereby altering the effective length of the vibrating segment, a process known as stopping. To excite the strings into vibration, they are normally stroked (*arco*) by a ribbon of horsehair mounted under tension on a suitable stick or bow. For special effects the strings may be 'plucked' by the fingers (*pizzicato*). In modern violin playing the natural overtones of the strings (*natural harmonics*) are also employed occasionally by touching the strings lightly with a finger at an appropriate fractional distance along the string and adjusting the bow pressure suitably. *Artificial harmonics* may also be generated by shortening the length of vibrating segment with firm pressure from the first finger of the left hand, accompanied by the light touch of the fourth finger at the appropriate point. *Vibrato,* which imparts some warmth to the tone, is accomplished by regular variations of pitch arising from appropriate tremulous movements of the left hand. Sounds arising from the vibration of the strings are reinforced by the vibrations of the body and the air cavity of the instrument.

It will be seen that there is some justification for saying that players of the violin family 'make their own notes'. They begin by tuning their strings usually in fifths apart and forming the intervening notes by altering the lengths of the vibrating segments by pressing the strings on the finger board.

In the pianoforte, sounds are again produced from strings but the pitch is not controlled by the performer.

Separate strings are provided for each note of the keyboard. Moreover to secure greater tonal intensity, from about GGG to BB each key has two strings tuned to unison, thus producing resonance effects and from about C upwards, three strings to a note (hence the term tri-chord action). By means of a suitable mechanical arrangement, the pianoforte strings are set into vibration by percussion from felted hammers actuated by the depression of the keys on the keyboard. The intensity and brilliancy of the tone depend upon the force of the hammer blow on the string, this depending in turn upon the degree of pressure exercised by the performer on the keyboard. Judged from this simple description, the pianoforte seems to be a purely mechanical instrument and some writers have thus been tempted to detract from its musical significance. This is however not the whole story (see p. 11).

Some forerunners of the pianoforte should be noted especially in view of their revival to-day in an attempt to secure historical authenticity in performance. In the harpsichord, stretched strings mounted horizontally are plucked; when a key on the keyboard (resembling that of the pianoforte) is depressed, a piece of wood (called a jack) carrying a projection of wood, metal or quill, is caused to rise vertically by means of a system of levers so that the projections pluck the strings. The jack then falls back by gravity. In this way tones with clear definition are produced, very suitable for part playing, but with little variation of intensity. Tone production in the virginals and spinet was similarly produced. In the clavichord the operation of the keys caused wedge-shaped pieces of metal to press on the strings thus dividing the strings into two segments. One segment was allowed to vibrate and produce a note of required pitch while the other segment remained silent by pressure of a piece of felt on it.

In the harp, strings of varied length are plucked by the

player. Each string must be tuned separately by adjusting its tension by means of a key or peg.

In a large group of instruments, sounds are made either from the vibration of air columns of appropriate length, e.g. flue organ pipes and the flute, or from the combination of air columns acting as resonators with some auxiliary tone originator, e.g. oboe, clarinet, reed organ pipes, orchestral brass and the human voice. A flue organ pipe contains a column of air in a tube. A stream of air of given pressure enters the foot of the pipe, and in escaping is caused to set the column of air into a steady state of vibration. If the top of the pipe is open, a complete series of overtones is produced—octave, twelfth, fifteenth, etc. If the top of the pipe is closed, then alternate overtones, the octave, fifteenth, nineteenth, etc. are absent and the tone is less bright than for the corresponding open pipe. The pitch of the notes of a pipe depends upon the length of the air column; the pitch of the fundamental of a stopped pipe is an octave lower than that of an open pipe having the same length of air column.

In the reed pipes of an organ, the original source of vibration is a short tongue of metal in the foot of the pipe whose length and weight determine the pitch of the note produced. Its tone is reinforced by the vibrations of the column of air in the pipe. Orchestral woodwind instruments such as the oboe, clarinet and bassoon act in the same way as reed pipes in an organ, being provided with a reed of cane in the mouthpiece to originate the sound.

Brass instruments may also be regarded as a coupled system, the lips of the player serving as originator of the vibrations and the air column in the tube as reinforcing the tone by resonance. The simple post horn, consisting of cup-shaped mouthpiece for the lips and a straight tube with bell end, is limited to the notes of the harmonic series and is therefore only suitable for sounding fanfares.

To obtain notes of the chromatic scale brass instruments in general employ side tubes which, by the operation of three or four valves, may be brought into the length of the main air column, thereby extending the simple series of tones of the post horn.

It should be noted that the human voice is similar in action to a reed pipe, the vocal cords serving as initial source of vibration with the cavities of the mouth and nose acting as resonators.

Little need be said about tone production in the percussion instruments of the orchestra—the cymbals, triangle, glockenspiel, drums, etc. as the source of sound is obvious. The drums may be tuned within a limited range of pitch by altering the tension of the skin or membrane.

The Reproduction of Musical Sounds

The three leading characteristics of a musical sound, pitch, loudness and quality, give rise to a complex wave-curve, Fig. 3, p. 47, representing the corresponding air movements during its transmission. Hence it follows that if a permanent record of this wave curve is made and some means of using this curve to reproduce the original air movements is available, reproduction of sound becomes possible. The now familiar gramophone disc carries in its spiral groove a track containing all the features of a sound wave curve. The needle of a gramophone explores this track and causes the diaphragm attached thereto to transmit to the air movements similar to those made by the original source of sound. The horn or loudspeaker serves to amplify the effect.

Recent improvements in the electrical recording of sounds eliminate much of the mechanical action of stylus on disc by electro-magnetic means using a microphone, thus avoiding the unpleasant scratchiness of early recording. Great advances are being made in this field of electrical engineering. The tape recorder for example makes use of variations of magnetic density on a moving wire or metal tape corresponding to fluctuations in the magnetising current, these in turn varying with the sound characteristics of the music being recorded. The latest development is the ionophone which 'radiates sound' from what is virtually a radio valve, thus by avoiding mechanical parts altogether, eliminating the mechanical defects that reduce the fidelity of the ordinary loudspeaker.

Tone Production by Electrical Means

synthetic tone

The complete vindication of the acoustical theory of overtones, transients, and formants is to be seen in the recent development of electrical musical instruments, which by entirely electrical means manufacture tones of distinctive quality either by combining pure tones to form a desired harmonic series or by filtering overtones from an initial harmonically rich tone (p. 45). The former method has been used with great success in the Compton Electrone, an electrotonic organ made by the John Compton Organ Company, London, in which electrostatic condensers of fluctuating capacity give rise to modulated electric currents resulting in the final production of pure tones; these are then synthesised in suitable proportions to form the tone colours desired, e.g. clarinet, trumpet, diapason, flute.

Some obvious advantages attach to electrotonic instruments, namely, their portability, their freedom from the necessity of frequent tuning, the possibility of disposing their tone cabinets at the most convenient points in the auditorium for the listener, and—with the Compton electrostatic instrument—even the overcoming of bad acoustics in the auditorium by simulating a substantial reverberation period. A disadvantage is that the final sounds come from loudspeakers whose deficiencies therefore set a limit to the musical effect. However, these draw-backs are likely soon to be overcome by the employment of the ionophone in place of loudspeakers (see p. 58). So far, electrotonic instruments have been mainly imitative but composers and orchestrators should not overlook the possibility of employing them for tone colours not covered by the existing orchestral range. Some careful experimental work is called for in this direction between composers and the instrument manufacturers.

Another electrical application employs the microphone to pick up sounds originating from mechanical vibrations say from strings or strips of metal specially mounted. In this way a rich series of overtones may be secured from which appropriate selections may be made corresponding to the tone colours desired. The Neo-Bechstein piano of pre-war days and the Wurlitzer Orgatron in the U.S.A. are examples of this application.

Some success has been achieved in the microphone pick-up and subsequent amplification of sounds from the usual musical instruments e.g. with a microphone in the swell box of an organ or near a pianoforte. In such cases an undesirable change of quality in the amplified sounds may often be detected thus limiting the application of the method.

VI

MUSICAL SOUNDS AND THE EAR

'Dischord ofte in musick makes the sweeter lay.'
Spenser

'Musick is of a relative nature, and what is harmony to one ear, may be dissonance to another.'
Addison: *The Spectator*

Hearing

Without going into physiological details we may note that the ear is an exceedingly complex structure capable of receiving the waves from a source of vibrations, analysing them and making its own contribution to the resulting mental effect—for again it must be emphasised that music is an activity of the mind. As to frequency, the ear might at first seem rather limited in range of response, from 20 c/s to 20,000 c/s, outside these limits no aural effect being obtained by direct impact of incoming waves; but it is still possible for the ear to perceive an effect due to combinations of frequencies outside this range, e.g. two frequencies of say 30,000 c/s and 25,000 c/s respectively would give a difference tone of 5,000 c/s falling within the range, thus showing that the response of the ear to incoming waves is eclectic. (The student who is interested in electricity may compare this with heterodyning).

The sensitivity of the ear to the intensity of sounds is quite remarkable. Alexander Wood expressed it in a striking way by analogy with the eye, namely, that the minimum energy detectable by the ear corresponds to that from a 50-watt electric lamp situated 3,000 miles away! It is this high sensitivity that makes possible the subtle dynamic effects in the phrasing and interpretation of music.

Sensitivity to melodic differences in pitch depends upon the particular part of the audibility range concerned, the ear being most sensitive to semitone steps in the middle of the pianoforte keyboard. At the bottom of the keyboard the ear is so insensitive that piano tuners often leave some of the notes untouched.

Loudness and Intensity; Frequency and Pitch

The early concentration of acoustical research upon purely physical phenomena obscured the most significant musical aspects of hearing. Until about twenty-five years ago the terms intensity and loudness, as also frequency and pitch, were used indiscriminately. Moreover, it was assumed without question that frequency and intensity were entirely independent categories. The pressure wave curve seemed to be a complete representation of the phenomena, the number of wave-lengths per unit along the axis corresponding to frequency and the heights of the ordinates representing intensity.

We now know that from the musical point of view this is entirely inadequate. The ear itself plays an important part in the process of hearing, going far beyond that of merely serving as a receiver of the incoming waves. This leads to the need for emphasising the physiological as well as the physical aspects of hearing, loudness and pitch being the terms employed for the aural effects.

Loudness and pitch are not independent of one another. There is an instrument called an audiometer which enables us to produce a sound of variable frequency and constant amplitude. Let us suppose therefore that this instrument is set to produce a sound of moderate but fixed amplitude corresponding of course to constant intensity according to simple physical theory. Now let the pitch be raised continuously from say 100 c/s to 10,000 c/s. Then in spite of the constant amplitude, it will be found that the loudness actually changes with the rise of pitch. At first, the loudness increases to a maximum in the region 3,000 c/s. From there the loudness *decreases* even though the pitch rises. We have assumed moderate degrees of loudness as for example in the notes of a pianoforte; for very loud sounds, the effect is still more complicated.

Another way of describing the effect is to say that the ear is most sensitive to the high pitched sounds and especially to those in the neighbourhood of 3,000 c/s (in the top octave of the pianoforte), hence we see the reason for the disparity in size between the violin and the double bass; the latter instrument must needs be capable of a large output of sound energy to compensate for the comparative insensitivity of the ear at its low pitch range.

Decibels and Phons

Psychologists have done considerable research on the nature of the relationship between the magnitudes of physical stimulus and the corresponding sensations produced. The results are summarised in *Weber's Law* which states that the increase in stimulus necessary to produce a just perceptible increase in sensation is proportional to the original stimulus. For normal hearing it is found that a change of about 25 per cent in stimulus is needed to distinguish differences in loudness between two notes. From *Weber's Law* a useful scale of intensity/loudness relations may be devised based upon a ten-fold increase in sound energy, namely:

Increase in loudness

1	2 times	3 times	4 times, etc.

Increase in energy

10 times	100 times	1,000 times	10,000 times, etc.
$= 10^1$	$= 10^2$	$= 10^3$	$= 10^4$

The lower limit is of course the threshold of hearing. The steps of loudness based upon this ten-fold increase in sound energy give a unit of intensity called the *bel* (from the name of Charles Graham Bell, a famous telephone engineer). This unit is rather large and is replaced in practice by a tenth of its value called the *decibel*.

The following table (which is approximate only) will give the reader some idea of the magnitude of a decibel:

Threshold of hearing	0	decibels
Violin, just audible	5–10	,,
Whisper	10–20	,,
Busy street	50–80	,,
Loud conversation	70	,,
London tube	70–90	,,
Full symphony orchestra, *ff*	80–90	,,
Pneumatic drill	110	,,
Threshold of pain	130	,,

To be strictly comparable the above sounds would need to be of the same pitch. Moreover, we must note that this is a table of intensities and not of differences in loudness, i.e. physical as against psychological. If we wish to compare sensations, we must have a different unit since loudness and intensity are not in exact correspondence and besides their relation is not the same at all pitches. The sensation unit is the *phon* taken at a pitch level corresponding to 1,000 c/s. On this scale a whisper is about 10 phons, the noise of an express train to a passenger about 60 phons, while a painfully loud sound is about 130 phons.

There is admittedly much confusion about these various units and their application—some writers using decibels and phons as interchangeable terms—reflecting considerable uncertainty in our knowledge of these complex aural phenomena. However, the day may yet come when the composer may employ phon-meter markings in his scores to secure a more faithful reproduction of his dynamic indications than is at present obtained from the aural range *pp* to *ff*.

In concluding this discussion on loudness reference may be made to its practical utility in organ playing. An intensity change from say large open diapason to 'full to 15th' may be so great that the quiet dulciana may be completely masked. Moreover the dynamic effect of high pitched stops is often much greater than their small scale may suggest—hence the discerning organist will often obtain considerable apparent increase in loudness by the addition of single high pitched stops rather than by piling on large masses of unison toned diapasons. Designers of organ specifications should also take notice of this principle which was certainly well known three centuries ago, as is evidenced by the designers of the so-called baroque organs.

Classic design [handwritten marginal note]

The Ear creates Sound

Tartini (1692-1770), the violinist, discovered that when two notes (called *generators*) such as G $= 384$ c/s and B $= 480$ c/s are sounded together, a third tone called the *resultant* may be distinctly heard accompanying them. The frequency of the resultant is equal to the *difference* between the frequencies of the generators. In the case cited it would be $480 - 384 = 96$ c/s which is two octaves below the lower of the two generators. Weaker difference tones of the second order may also be detected arising from the combination of the first difference tone (96 c/s) and either of its generators for example, $384 - 96 = 288$ c/s.

Tartini called the resultant tones *terzi suoni* (third sounds) but they are often called 'Tartini tones'. The

German organist, Sorge (1703-1778), had also noticed their occurrence and was led to develop from them a resultant 32 ft tone, the acoustic 32 ft stop on the organ, by combining in pairs pipes from 16 ft ranks played in fifths e.g. CCC = 32 c/s sounded simultaneously with GGG = 48 c/s gives the first order difference tone 48 — 32 = 16 c/s = CCCC, which latter is the fundamental tone from an open organ pipe 32 ft long.

Besides these differences, two simultaneous sounds give *summation* tones by the sum of the frequencies of the generators e.g. C = 128 c/s together with G = 192 c/s gives the first order tone E = 320 c/s. Summation tones are in general much weaker than difference tones but there is no doubt that taken together they greatly enhance the harmonic effect of sounds produced simultaneously. It is generally agreed that both difference and summation tones are *subjective* phenomena and that we are justified in saying that the ear creates them from the incoming sounds. Much research still remains to be done on these and other related subjective phenomena.

Consonance and Dissonance

The mental effects arising from simultaneously occurring sounds play a substantial part in modern music. While various levels of agreeability between sounds are recognised, nevertheless two clearly defined kinds of combination stand out, namely, concords and discords. Consonance and dissonance are distinguished from each other according to the degree of intensity of the beats between the constituent tones. Consideration of the number of beats per second between pairs of tones low in pitch, and high in pitch, respectively, will readily show that even the same interval may sound more consonant in some parts of the tonal range than in others; the student should listen carefully to the effect of a major third played in different parts of the range of a pianoforte or organ. Moreover, the dissonance of a given interval varies according to its degree of loudness as seen for example in some modern impressionistic music for the pianoforte. Since each musical sound is in itself a complex structure of overtones we would expect a complicated beating effect between the overtones when two or more sounds are produced simultaneously (p. 31). The closer two tones are together, the more pronounced are the beats, hence the rougher effect of small intervals like tones and semitones when compared with wide-spaced fourths, fifths and octaves.

Figure 5 shows the tonal structure of the octave, fifth and third respectively in terms of overtones, difference tones and summation tones. The extreme consonance of the octaves as compared with the interval of a third is obvious. It is a useful exercise for the student to show in

Fig. 5. Illustrates the structure of intervals: (a) octave; (b) perfect fifth; (c) major third. Generating tones (semibreves); overtones (minims); difference tones, first order (crotchets); second order (quavers); summation tones (semiquavers).

the same manner the resultant structure from combinations of notes in triads and other chords. In this way some of the rules of elementary harmony will be seen to have an acoustical foundation. Nevertheless the student is warned against acoustical theories of harmony. Experience shows that purely physical theories are sterile. All they can do is to give explanations for the elementary phenomena of roughness and smoothness of intervals. It is not their province to account for musical preferences.

Important recent studies have emphasised that the principle of tonal relatedness (p. 12) cannot be ignored even in the field of consonance or dissonance for it has been shown that the degree of consonance or dissonance of a given combination of sounds depends upon its musical context. Such a result should make clear the narrowness of the traditional acoustics which was concerned only with tones or intervals in isolation.

VII

THE STUDIO AND CONCERT HALL

'. . . that branching roof
Self-poised, and scooped into ten thousand cells,
Where light and shade repose, where music dwells
Lingering—and wandering on as loth to die;
Like thoughts whose very sweetness yieldeth proof
That they were born for immortality.'
Wordsworth:
Sonnet on King's College Chapel, Cambridge

The Acoustical Problem

Our original picture of the sequence of processes involved in the production of sounds is essentially simple in character, namely, a source of vibration such as a musical instrument, a medium (usually the air surrounding the source, which serves to transmit energy in the form of waves) and finally the ear of the listener which receives the waves. From the musical standpoint, this picture is altogether too crude, for among other things it fails to take into account what may happen to the sound waves from the time they are produced by the vibrations of the source to the instant when they are received by the ear—if indeed they reach the ear, since under certain circumstances it is quite possible for the waves to be obliterated, or dispersed, or diverted so that they fail to reach the ear.

Until musicians made known their requirements for a satisfactory performance, physicists paid little attention to the function of the medium other than to describe *how* it comes about that the medium transmits sound waves by a series of compressions and rarefactions. Hence it happened that the early concert halls and studios were of haphazard acoustical properties. Occasionally a hall would be favourable to music, but more often concert halls were entirely unsympathetic to the performer, thus the tone would appear lifeless or attenuated and difficult to produce. Even the same hall would show great divergency in acoustical effect when filled with an audience from its qualities when empty. Clearly, from the performer's point of view it is most unsatisfactory that despite the excellence of his technique and interpretation, the musical result may be valueless merely because the external conditions of the performance are unsuitable— conditions over which the performer has no control. This leads us to consider the desiderata for a satisfactory concert hall.

Examination of the remains of arenas and auditoriums of ancient times, particularly those of the Greeks and Romans, indicates that certain general acoustical properties of buildings were well known to them, for example, the laws of the reflection of sound waves and the bearing of the shape of the building on the dispersion of sound waves; it is certain too that the ancient builders were acquainted with the focusing properties of oval-shaped walls and the resonating qualities of cavities. The directional properties of sound boards was also known as may be seen in some of the buildings erected under the supervision of Vitruvius, author of the first systematic treatise on Architecture, *De Architectura,* written in the First Century B.C.

We have no record, however, that ancient builders had more than an empirical knowledge of building acoustics acquired mainly through imitation of natural forms such as the shell, in much the same way as, it is said, the excellent qualities of the Mormon Tabernacle at Salt Lake City were achieved. The story goes that, when the

Tabernacle was first projected, the builders inquired of their great leader, Brigham Young, what shape it should be made and he replied that the inside of an egg is a perfect form hence the ceiling should take its shape from nature. It is only 50 years since the principles of acoustical design of buildings have been satisfactorily recognised, enabling one to design a building *in advance* with certainty that it shall be entirely suitable for the performance of music or for effective speech. This development involves entirely new knowledge coupled with ancient practice on the reflection and dispersion of sound.

Pioneer discoverer in the new knowledge was Professor Sabine of Harvard University, U.S.A., who was asked to assist in ensuring that a new concert hall to be built in the University should be adequate to its purpose. He set himself the problem of finding the criterion which determined what it is that makes a room good or bad for speech or music and found the answer in what he called the *reverberation period,* namely, the time taken for a sound of moderate loudness, and pitch about that of the middle of the pianoforte keyboard, to die away when the source stops vibrating. It has of course long been known that a rough test of the acoustic qualities of a room could be made by producing a sudden sharp sound such as clapping the hands and noticing whether or not the sound stopped suddenly or lingered on. Bach is said to have been a good judge of building acoustics and applied some such test when called in to advise on the erection of new organs in churches or improving existing installations.

Reverberation Period

To understand fully the significance of this term it is necessary to consider for a moment what happens in the air when a sound is made. Whatever may be the vibrating source, for example, the human voice or an instrument, waves of compression are sent out through the air in all directions. These will soon meet the walls, ceiling, floor and objects in the room since the sound travels at 1,100 feet per second. *The acoustic properties of the room are determined by what happens to the waves at the various surfaces which it meets.* Thus, if the surfaces of the walls are smooth and hard, the sound waves will be almost totally reflected, that is to say, there will be little loss in their energy. The reflected waves will then in their turn be reflected again and again from the walls. Since the loss in their energy is only slight at each reflection, a considerable time elapses before they are so reduced in intensity as to be unable to affect the ear. In other words if the walls and ceiling and objects in the room are good reflectors of sound, the sound waves will persist for a considerable interval of time, for example, in St Paul's Cathedral this interval is of the order 10 seconds. In a theatre, it will usually be about 1—2 seconds.

Considerations such as these lead to the classification of materials used in building and furnishing a room according to their ability to *absorb* sound waves; good absorbers are bad reflectors and *vice versa*. Thus it comes about that a studio which has a thick pile carpet and is heavily draped with curtains will absorb sounds readily and have a small reverberation period; in consequence, to a performer it will have a deadening effect upon the sounds he produces.

In recent years the absorptive powers of most materials have been measured and the results made available to architects and builders in lists of *absorption coefficients* which show the degree of absorption of each material when compared with the 'absorption' of an open window. Clearly, if the sound waves meet an open window, they are immediately lost, which is another way of saying that they are completely absorbed, hence the open window is taken as a standard and its absorption coefficient is unity. Carpeting materials have a coefficient about 0·5 (the exact value depends on the texture), meaning that half the energy of the incoming sound waves is absorbed at each reflection. Glass is a very good reflector, being smooth and hard, so we are not surprised to find that its absorption coefficient is small, only 0·01 or less.

We have not yet explained why excessive absorption accompanied by a short reverberation period should produce an acoustically 'dead' room. The reason depends on the important fact that waves of short wave-length are more readily absorbed than those of long wave-length, that is, notes of high pitch are extinguished more quickly than those of low pitch. Hence, the high pitched overtones in musical sounds are the first to suffer absorption. Since brilliancy of tone depends almost entirely on these, their loss is immediately noticeable to the performer in a lack of liveliness in his tone production.

The following table shows how absorption and pitch are connected. Absorption coefficients should strictly be given for stated pitches but in practice (as above) they are usually taken to refer to notes in the middle of the pianoforte keyboard in the absence of more specific information on pitch.

ABSORPTION COEFFICIENTS (*Approximate values*)

Materials	Frequency	
	500 c/s	3000 c/s
(Open Window)	1·0	1·0
Brick	0·03	0·05
Glass	0·03	0·05
Carpets	0·50	0·70
Felt	0·60	0·90
Plaster	0·02	0·04
Acoustic plaster (various)	0·20-0·40	0·20-0·50

Performers in concert halls are well acquainted with the acoustic difference between an empty hall and the same hall when filled with a compact audience. The absorptive power of the latter is notoriously high. Even for sounds of moderate pitch it is estimated that each adult is equivalent to about 5 square feet of open window!

Besides absorption, Sabine found that the *volume* of the auditorium had an important effect on the reverberation period, large halls being more reverberant than those of small capacity. Assembling all the information, he showed the dependence of the reverberation period on the various factors by the following formula:

$$T = \frac{0{\cdot}05\ V}{\Sigma\ aS}$$

Here, T is the absorption period in seconds. V is the volume of the hall in cubic feet. The denominator on the right is 'the sum of' (denoted by the Greek letter *sigma,* Σ) the products of the areas (in square feet) of each surface exposed to the sound waves into its corresponding absorption coefficient *a*.

The significance of this relationship for architectural acoustics cannot be overestimated. It means that no longer need the acoustical properties of a proposed new concert hall be a matter of chance. It means also that once the purpose of the hall is stated the architect may specify the size of the hall and the materials of its surfaces and know *in advance* what acoustical effects the hall will possess. The recent erection of the Royal Festival Hall in London (1951) is a splendid vindication of this modern knowledge of architectural acoustics.

What is the Optimum Reverberation Period?

Having shown how the acoustical properties of a studio or concert hall are determined by purely objective factors subject to the control and specification of the architect and builder, we now pass on to those elusive desiderata of the performer and listener—elusive because we are no longer dealing with objective but with subjective factors. Sabine has enabled us to design a hall with a pre-determined reverberation period. Now the question arises, how big must we make the reverberation period? A large period tends to make music blurred and to render it difficult to pick out the meaning from speech, thus, if the period were 4 seconds and a speaker produced his words at the rate of 2 syllables a second the listener would have to piece together his meaning from 8 syllables 'in the air' at a time! A short period therefore favours clarity whether of music or speech. But to carry this to its apparent logical conclusion and suggest that the period should be zero is not allowable for then we should get a room that is 'dead'. A slight continuation of the sound after the source has stopped vibrating is usually felt to be desirable to give life to the performance, thus making the hall resonant as it is sometimes called. (It should be noted that we are considering the direct effect of performances in halls and studios upon a listener; we exclude the special case of radio transmission from studios when microphonic conditions may demand complete lack of resonance, and therefore zero period.)

Attempts have been made to reduce the determination of the optimum reverberation period to a formula according to the size of the hall being designed but this appears to be pressing a too rigid objective standard on what after all is subjective. It is perhaps better to recognise that the optimum period depends on the particular use to which the hall is to be put. For music, a large hall might well have a period of up to two seconds, whereas for speech, a period of only one second would be desirable. To meet varying needs, the hall might be provided with interchangeable absorption panels so as to adapt the period to its special purpose as is done for example in the broadcasting concert hall at Copenhagen.

The whole question however is an aesthetic one. When the architect says he is setting out to 'reform' public taste by imposing small reverberation periods so that excessive clarity shall result we must call a halt. Surely, this is a matter for the musician to decide. In the case of large scale vocal and instrumental performances, a time lag may often produce a significant and desirable musical effect. Indeed, even a small time lag gives rise to a binding together of the music, and produces a unifying intellectual effect. It is seemingly a matter for the individual whether this integration of phrase is preferred to single note clarity in contrapuntal music, hence the decided differences of opinion on the merits of various halls. But the Royal Festival Hall, with its low period, does not necessarily out-place the Royal Albert Hall. Admittedly, however, there is such a thing as *aural conditioning*—'the ear can get used to anything', it is truly said.

Even when the reverberation period has been satisfactorily determined another factor of great importance to the comfort of listeners must be considered, namely, the need for uniformity in the distribution of the sound. In one recently built hall one must choose one's seat with caution for an orchestral concert. At certain locations, while the violins are excessively brilliant, the double basses can scarcely be heard with the result that the tonal structure of the music is entirely destroyed. This is due to uneven distribution of sound from the widely spaced orchestral forces. To improve the effect, large judiciously placed reflecting surfaces are needed to change the original directional properties of the hall.

Then again some halls with curved walls or perhaps a domed roof exercise peculiar focusing effects which can be very distressing to the serious listener. It is to avoid this kind of result that careful architects test out their designs in advance of building by constructing shallow troughs into which mercury is placed, the sides of the troughs being shaped according to various sections taken across the drawings of the proposed building. Ripples are made on the surface of the mercury from a vibrating tuning fork. They spread over the surface till they reach the boundary walls where they are reflected. A careful examination of the reflected waves will thus show by analogy what is likely to happen to sound waves reflected from the walls of the hall of which the troughs are scaled models.

Advanced planning of this kind cannot be too strongly advocated.

How to improve a defective hall or studio

Let us consider first the hall that is 'dead' to the performer. This results from too small a reverberation period depending in turn on the extent of absorption and the volume of the room. Clearly, nothing substantial can be done about altering the volume of the room, except in cases like that of a church where the removal of an oppressive gallery produced consequent improvement in resonance. Reduction of absorbent materials remains to be done. Heavy curtains, thick pile carpets and felts should be avoided. Every effort should be made to provide extensive hard reflecting surfaces. Even so, the final effect may not be entirely satisfactory due of course to the physical limitations. It is easier to deal with the too resonant room. Experiments with suitably placed absorbing material will usually result in a reduction of reverberation period. A word must be said here regarding special absorbing plasters and composition panels now available in a series of grades of sound absorption thus enabling wall surfaces to be modified to secure the most appropriate degree of absorption. These open up new acoustical possibilities since panels giving degrees of absorption may be interchanged according to the demand of the music or speech to be performed.

When all has been done to secure the needed improvement in reverberation period it only remains to experiment with reflecting panels for effective projection of the sound waves. The soundboard over a church pulpit is a case in point.

Reference must also be made to the treatment of the organ in poor acoustic buildings. We have already observed that a non-resonant building results in loss of brilliancy due to the absorption of the higher members of the series of overtones. To overcome this, organ builders deliberately increase the number of mutation and mixture stops in the specification of an organ for a deficient building and strengthen their tonal output, thus to a high degree simulating the needed brilliancy. The treatment of the mixture work in the organ of Leeds Parish Church is a splendid example of this method.

The Hall and the Performer

The terms 'live' and 'dead', so frequently used in reference to halls, express the effect which they have upon music and speech. For a given set of external conditions, the performer must adapt himself to produce as effective a result as possible. With a resonant hall, that is, one having a long reverberation period, in the interests of clarity he will need to play more slowly than in one that is less resonant. Organists are of course well acquainted with this necessity when performing in lofty resonant churches. Then again, stage and platform draperies must be taken into account. A solo performer would be well advised to take up a position well forward to reduce curtain absorption to a minimum. For the same reason it is never entirely satisfactory to stand on a carpet. The placing of an orchestra or choir on a heavily curtained stage needs great care if members at the back and sides are not to be rendered ineffective, not to speak of the sound energy being lost into the ceiling. Quite often, too, performers find that a platform with a roof girder over the length of its front edge constitutes a sound trap that reduces their tonal volume by a large percentage— another reason for standing well forward.

VIII

THE MEANS OF MUSICAL EXPRESSION

'The soul of music slumbers in the shell,
Till waked and kindled by the master's spell.'
Samuel Rogers (1763-1855)

The Principle of Artistic Deviation

We have already indicated that the borderline between the physical and psychological aspects of music is somewhat diffuse. The new musical acoustics, while giving due importance to the physical phenomena does not neglect the psychological implications. It often happens too that phenomena that are plainly psychological in origin may be given some measure of objective physical explanation. The application of purely acoustical and mechanical knowledge has provided the means for a wide range of tones as seen in the various musical instruments. What use is made of these clearly demands a directing mind.

It cannot be too strongly emphasised that music is an activity of the mind whether it be in the composer's origination of various combinations of sounds or in the performer's actual production of sounds by means of an instrument. Musical performance is characterised by the most outstanding circumstance that it is never in any real sense exact. Its departure from exactness is indeed the criterion of its mental origin. As soon as it becomes exact it passes over into the mechanical and so ceases to be

79

accepted as musical. A mechanical piano is (musically speaking) condemned by its name.

Musical performances are never in strict time, or at uniform intensity level, indeed the appropriateness of the deliberate deviations by the performer from mechanical strictness is used in assessing the extent of his artistry. Every performance is thus seen to be unique. In passing it should be noted that attempts to provide an objective assessment of artistry by measuring the amounts of departure from strictness have failed, for who is to say whether this or that amount of deviation is artistic?

Here we shall content ourselves with noting a few simple ways in which the performer is assisted physically in securing artistic deviations through the special use of modifications or additions to his instrument.

The Pianoforte

Strict time is not a characteristic of good performance as is seen in the examination of the rolls made by master pianists for the player-piano, there being marked variations in the relative values of notes and even in the durations of the bars. Changes in intensity are used to impart expression to phrases, the sustaining pedal being particularly valuable for this purpose. It is a device enabling the normal dampers to be raised from the strings which are thus free to vibrate. In conjunction with suitable key attack a melody may be made extremely expressive thereby.

Half-pedalling, a rapid up and down movement of the sustaining pedal, enables changing harmonies over a sustained bass note to be achieved, since the inertia of the heavy bass strings does not allow them to respond immediately to the damper action when the pedal comes up only momentarily. The action of a modern pianoforte is that of a precision tool permitting great subtlety of tonal effects in phrasing and accentuation when passing from note to note or tone to tone by an almost unlimited series of gradations in touch from *legatissimo* to *staccatissimo*. It should be noted that the pianoforte is essentially a percussion instrument. No advantage therefore attaches to pressing the keys after sounds have been made, indeed, such key-bedding leads to faulty technique.

The Organ

The characteristic property of an organ is to sustain sounds indefinitely in which respect it is therefore opposed to the pianoforte. Expression by means of intensity changes is rather illusory. Some of the pipes are enclosed in a box of which one or more sides may be opened or closed by the player to enable the sounds to come out more freely or *vice versa* thus simulating *crescendo* and *diminuendo*. Apart from this means, phrasing and accentuation are achieved subjectively through the judicious employment of key release at the end of a phrase and beginning the next phrase in strict time.

A wide range of tone colours is provided in the organ from appropriate kinds of pipe—diapason, flute, clarinet, trumpet, etc. Brilliancy of tone may be achieved by the use of special ranks of pipes called mutations and mixtures to emphasise the overtones. The builder also makes use of heavy wind pressures to secure brilliancy and power.

Recently, attention has been drawn to the advantages of the organs of the 15th, 16th and 17th centuries which were characterised by low wind pressures, small pipe scales and a plentiful supply of mutations and mixtures. These were excellent for part-playing in fugues. Loudness was achieved not so much from the use of powerful wind pressures at unison pitches as by the subjective effects from high pitched stops operating at the most sensitive level of the ear.

The tones from unenclosed organ pipes have often been described as cold and unemotional. A certain warmth may be imparted to the tones by slight regular fluctuations in pitch. This is an expressive device well known in violin playing and singing when it is called *vibrato*. Used with critical judgment it can be a valuable means of artistic deviation. On the organ, however, the vibrato or *tremolo* as it is called, must necessarily be mechanical and to this extent its artistic use is greatly restricted. The tremulant by which the tremolo is effected is a device for altering the wind supply to the pipes by regular small fluctuations —it is the uncontrollable regularity that restricts its artistic use. The injudicious use of the tremulant in cinema organs is largely responsible for their disrepute.

Warmth of tone may be imparted to the string-toned stops of the organ by deliberately tuning two ranks of pipes to be slightly out of tune with each other thereby creating beats. Again the effect is mechanical and must be judiciously used if it is to be artistic (p. 31).

The Violin

In this instrument the vibrato may contribute most artistically to performance for its extent and frequency of oscillation are entirely under the control of the player. Beats up to about seven per second yield satisfactory results with a pitch range of not more than a semitone on either side.

Though in general the quality of the tone of a violin is fixed, some significant changes may be made according to the 'position' in which notes are placed e.g. B, C, D first position on the A string or fifth position on the D string. Similarly in a scalewise passage it may make for a more uniform effect to avoid including an open string note since the notes from open strings are richer in overtones than those from stopped segments.

The Human Voice

The expressiveness of the human voice is legendary, being capable of endless artistic deviations. On the other hand, the vibrato may be greatly overdone; great restraint is needed to secure appropriate variations in pitch coupled with controlled frequency otherwise an inartistic 'wobble' results.

Considerable research is being done on the production of sounds by the human voice. Of special interest to singers is the recent experimental verification of a fact concerning vowel sounds that had previously only been a matter of surmise, namely, that each vowel sound is characterised by two particular frequencies of fixed pitch, one low, the other relatively high; for example:

a (as in f*a*ther)	825 c/s;	1200 c/s
u (as in m*oo*n)	400 c/s;	800 c/s
a (as in t*a*me)	550 c/s;	2100 c/s
e (as in s*ee*m)	375 c/s;	2400 c/s
a (as in c*a*p)	750 c/s;	1800 c/s

It is thus seen that both *oo* and *ee* sounds involve a low pitch, which explains the difficulty that soprano voices experience with these vowel sounds in their upper ranges. Recent work connected with telephony has brought out other interesting aspects of vocal tone production which may be briefly summarised by saying that the pitch of notes is determined by the vibration of the vocal cords; the vowel sounds are conditioned by the cavities of the pharynx and the mouth; the richness and quality of the voice is determined in the main by the head resonances arising from the various cavities, nasal and sinus. It is of interest that modern experiments seem to support the method of teaching singing known as *bel canto*; a rich field of suggestion awaits the enterprising teacher in the application of the new acoustical results to vocal technique.

BIBLIOGRAPHY

The student who wishes to pursue the subject further will find the following books particularly helpful:

Alexander Wood: *The Physics of Music* (London; Methuen, 1945; New York, Dover).

Cecil Forsyth: *Orchestration* (London; Macmillan, Stainer & Bell, 1948).

Frank Howes: *Full Orchestra* (London; Secker & Warburg, several editions).

Alan Douglas: *Electronic Musical Instrument Manual* (London; Pitman, 1949).

H. Lowery: *The Background of Music* (London; Hutchinson's University Library, 1952).
Discusses both the psychological and educational aspects of acoustics.

Thurston Dart: *The Interpretation of Music* (London; Hutchinson's University Library, 1954).

Robert Donington: *The Instruments of Music* (London; Methuen & Co., 1949).
Contains excellent detailed descriptions of musical instruments.

EXAMINATION QUESTIONS

Music students preparing for an examination in Acoustics may find the following questions of service. They are taken mainly from the examination papers of Trinity College of Music, London, by kind permission of Dr W. Greenhouse Allt, Principal of the College.

1. Explain the difference between *noise* and a *musical tone*.
2. State the source of vibration in the following cases:
   (a) flue organ pipe, (b) clarinet, (c) the human voice, (d) trumpet, (e) aeroplane, (f) the buzzing of a bee, (g) clapping the hands, (h) cymbals.
3. What are the wave-lengths of bottom C and top C on the pianoforte? (Assume the velocity of sound = 1,100 ft. per second and the frequency of middle C = 256 cycles per second.)
4. What is the frequency of a note of wave-length 8 ft.? (Assume the velocity of sound = 1,100 ft. per second.)
5. Sketch the wave form corresponding to a pure tone. In the same diagram add a second curve to represent a pure tone an octave higher than the first and of less intensity.
6. Sketch the wave form of a complex tone.
7. Under what conditions are beats produced? What are the frequencies of the two notes that will make four beats per second with a note of frequency 256 cycles per second?
8. A cog wheel has 24 teeth. At what rate must it rotate if the note produced by a card touching its toothed edge has a frequency of 360 cycles?
9. State the Principle of Resonance. Give three illustrations of the application of this principle in practical music.
10. Why do notes of the same pitch vary in quality according to the instrument on which they are produced?

11. Define the terms (a) overtone, (b) harmonic series, (c) difference tone, (d) summation tone, (e) acoustic spectrum.
12. Account for the difference in quality between the note from the open A string of a violin and the same note produced by stopping the D string with the fourth finger in the first position.
13. Account for the brilliancy of the *natural harmonics* played on the violin.
14. State the frequencies of the first three overtones of middle D = 288 cycles on the pianoforte.
15. Describe the production of sound by the human voice.
16. 'The human voice and a reed organ pipe operate according to the same physical principle.' Explain this.
17. Name the essential parts of the human vocal apparatus and state their functions.
18. Draw diagrams to represent the vertical sections of the flue and reed pipes of an organ respectively.
19. What is meant by the *speaking length* of a flue organ pipe? How are the wave-lengths of the fundamental and overtones of an *open* organ pipe related to the speaking length?
20. What are the frequencies of the first three overtones of an *open* organ pipe of fundamental frequency 96 cycles?
21. State the frequencies of the first three overtones of a *stopped* organ pipe of fundamental frequency 120 cycles.
22. Why do flue organ pipes go out of tune with change of temperature?
23. 'Flue pipes sharpen, reeds flatten with rise in temperature.' Explain this statement.
24. How are musical intervals expressed physically? Give a brief account of the interval relations in the natural diatonic scale and show how the equally tempered scale differs from the natural scale.
25. Define the term *equal temperament*. Describe the advantages and disadvantages of keyboard instruments tuned to *equal temperament*. Mention other methods of tuning that have been used in keyboard instruments.
26. What are Chladni's figures? Sketch examples of these

figures for a square plate and a circular plate respectively.

27. State the laws of transverse vibration of strings and show how they may be exemplified by reference either to the piano or the violin.

28. How does the frequency of the note from a stretched string vary with (a) the length of the vibrating segment and (b) the tension?

29. Describe how sound is transmitted through the air.

30. Explain the production of (a) natural harmonics, (b) artificial harmonics, on the violin.

31. When the note G is played on the D string of a violin, the G string may be seen to vibrate at the same time though not being bowed. How do you account for this?

32. Of three notes, the interval between the first and second is 4/3 and between the second and third 8/5. What is the interval between the first and third?

33. Give a brief account of the part played by the ear in practical music.

34. The energy of a musical tone is increased 10,000 times. By how much is the loudness increased?

35. If it is required to increase the loudness of a tone three times, by how much must the energy be increased?

36. Write a brief account of the measurement of the loudness of sounds and define the term *decibel*.

37. 'Some concert halls are good for sound while others are bad.' Comment on this statement and describe briefly the desiderata of a hall suitable for music.

38. What is meant by the *reverberation period* of an auditorium? Upon what factors does it depend? Suggest a method for reducing the value of the period in a very resonant room.

39. State the musical intervals between the fundamental and seven overtones respectively of a vibrating string. If the frequency of the fundamental is 200 cycles, what are the frequencies of these seven overtones?

40. What effect has the shape of a concert hall upon the distribution of sound?

41. Explain the effect of a sound-board in a hall.

42. Explain the terms (a) transients, (b) formants, in respect of the production of sound by musical instruments.
43. Describe the principle underlying any one type of
44. Give an account of the physical principles underlying the electrotonic organ.
    reproduction of sound by a gramophone.
45. Describe the construction of the piano referring especially to (a) the location of the points of impact of the hammers on the strings, (b) the fact that the bass strings are wrapped with spirals of wire and that (c) some notes have three strings in unison.
46. Write a brief essay on the physical aspects of consonance and dissonance.

ANSWERS

(3) Bottom C = 32 c/s. Wave-length = 34 ft. $4\frac{1}{2}$ ins.
     Top C = 4,096 c/s. Wave-length = 3 ins. approx.
(4) Wave-length = 8 ft. Frequency = 137.5 c/s.
(7) 260 c/s; 252 c/s.
(8) 15 revolutions per second.
(14) 1st overtone = 576 c/s; 2nd = 864 c/s; 3rd = 1,152 c/s.
(20) 1st overtone = 192 c/s; 2nd = 288 c/s; 3rd = 384 c/s.
(21) 1st overtone = 360 c/s; 2nd = 600 c/s; 3rd = 840 c/s.
(32) 32/15.
(34) Four times.
(35) One thousand times.
(39) Octave; twelfth; fifteenth; seventeenth (tierce); nineteenth (larigot); flat twenty-first; twenty-second. 400 c/s; 600 c/s; 800 c/s; 1,000 c/s; 1,200 c/s; 1,400 c/s; 1,600 c/s.

INDEX